ORKNEY'S
Italian
CHAPEL

Also by Philip Paris

The Italian Chapel
Men Cry Alone
Nylon Kid of the North
Trouble Shooting for Printers

For the last thirty years Philip Paris has worked in journalism and public relations. His quest to tell the story behind the Italian Chapel began in 2005 when he went to Orkney on honeymoon. During more than four years of research he has tracked down ex-POWs from the World War Two camps on Orkney as well as descendants of the key artists involved in building the chapel and those involved in running Camp 60. He lives in the Scottish Highlands.

ORKNEY'S *Italian* CHAPEL

THE TRUE STORY OF AN ICON

PHILIP PARIS

BLACK & WHITE PUBLISHING

First published 2010

This edition first published 2013

by Black & White Publishing Ltd

29 Ocean Drive, Edinburgh EH6 6JL

1 3 5 7 9 10 8 6 4 2   13 14 15 16

ISBN: 978 1 84502 529 8

Copyright © Philip Paris 2010, 2013

CONTENTS

ACKNOWLEDGEMENTS

Ken Amer, John Andrew, Molly Arbuthnott, Sam Moore Barlow, Anne Baxter, Mike Cameron, Camp Atterbury Veterans' Memorial Museum, Coriolano 'Gino' Caprara, Ged Clapson, Father Antony Collins, Alastair and Anne Cormack, Guido DeBonis, Margaret De Vitto, Mary Doyle, Gina Ellis, Eddie Farrell, Alfie Flett, Kim Foden, Letizia Fonti, Gary Gibson, David Goodman, Alison Sutherland Graeme, Robert Hall, Margaret Hogarth, Fran Flett Hollinrake, Alf Hutcheon, Rosemay Johnstone, Jon Meirion Jones, Phyllis Lemoncello, Peter MacDonald, David Mackie, Agnes McBarron, Lesley McLetchie, Willie Mowatt MBE, John Muir, Tom Muir, Tom O'Brien, *Orcadian*, Orkney Library, Giuseppe 'Pino' Palumbi, Renato Palumbi, Marlaine Payne, Roberto Pendini, Alberto Pizzi, John Orr, Manuela Re, Dr Francis Roberts, Iain Ross, Father Berardo Rossi, Harry Russell, Norman Sinclair, Tom Sinclair, James Thomson, United Churches of Chambersburg, Father Ronald Walls, Sheena Wenham, Aidan Weston-Lewis, Gale Winskill, Alistair Wivell, Fiona Zeyfert . . . and, of course, to my wife Catherine for her constant support, advice, help and love.

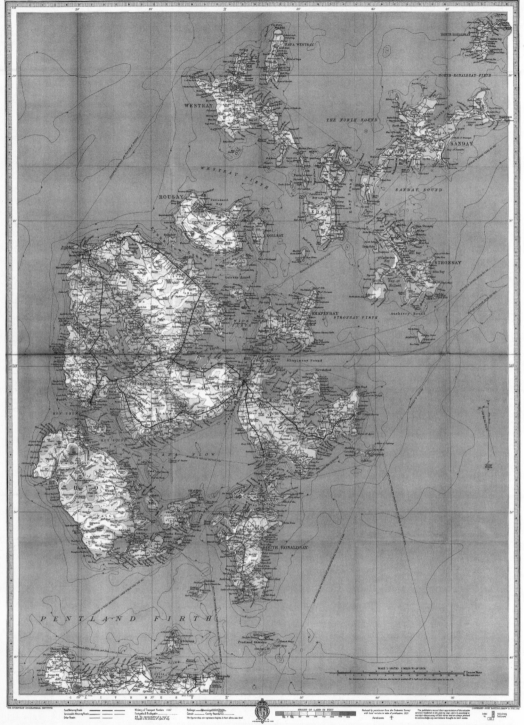

SCAPA FLOW DETAIL

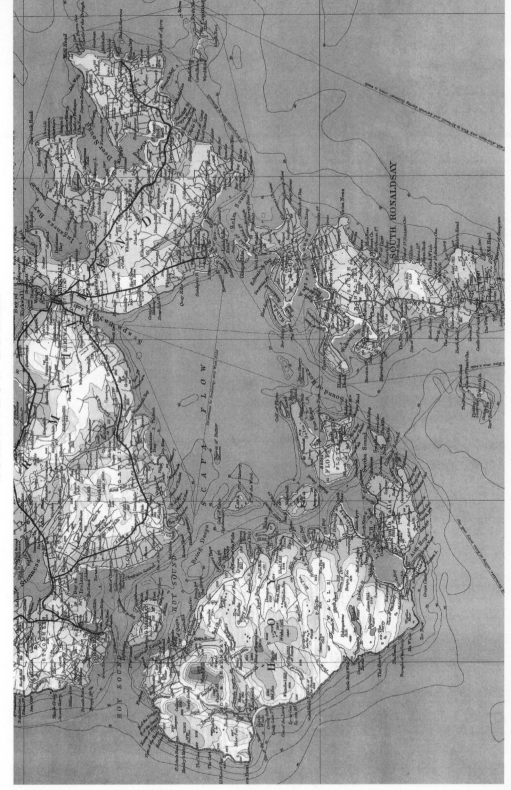

To Domenico Chiocchetti, who based his masterpiece of the Madonna and Child on a simple prayer card that he carried throughout the war; to Giuseppe Palumbi, who toiled for months at a forge to create a beautiful wrought iron rood screen; to Domenico Buttapasta, who transformed the outside of an ugly Nissen hut with a stunning façade; to Giovanni Pennisi, who modelled a bas-relief of the face of Christ; to Michele De Vitto and Assunto Micheloni, who installed power so that men could work, and pray, without interruption; and to the men who laboured, raised money and foraged for scrap materials . . . to create one of the greatest symbols of hope and peace to come out of the Second World War.

Introduction:
Discovering the Chapel

Entering the chapel on the tiny Orkney island of Lamb Holm on the third day of our honeymoon, Catherine and I had no idea that the visit would change our lives. It was 23rd August 2005. We were alone. The sun streamed in through the south-facing side windows, lighting up the inside so that the detail on the walls was both clear and clean; the dust particles hung in the air, unmoving in the stillness.

I knew nothing of the chapel's history other than that it had been built by Italian prisoners of war during the Second World War. I didn't know the Italians had been captured in North Africa after months of 'cat and mouse' fighting between Montgomery and Rommel. I didn't know they had arrived on a barren island in the winter of 1942, swapping the searing desert heat for the fierce Orkney weather.

The Italians may have escaped the danger of battle, but where had they arrived? Who among them had ever heard of these islands in the north of Scotland? Why had they been sent so far from home? It was to be a long time before I understood how these men overcame despair and loneliness to create a monument to the ability of the human spirit to rise above extreme hardship and hurt; the monument in which we now stood.

But despite knowing nothing more than that the chapel had been built by POWs, Catherine and I sensed something of what had been achieved by its creation. We each carried the booklet that was available at the entrance. Neither of us spoke as we walked towards the chancel and gazed upon the images; the angels and cherubim, the white dove, the four apostles. Our eyes were drawn constantly to the image above the altar; Domenico Chiocchetti's masterpiece of the Madonna and Child.

I rested my hand upon one of the gates in the centre of the beautiful rood screen, not realising that years later I would become friends with the grandson of the blacksmith, Giuseppe Palumbi, nor that the intricate wrought ironwork held a secret of forbidden love.

The building was silent . . . peaceful. It was a feeling I had never come close to experiencing in any of the grand cathedrals I had visited around Europe.

We started to read our booklets, which told of the 'Miracle of Camp 60'. In a way, the miracle was perhaps not the building itself, but how it gave hope to men despairing of life, and brought former enemies together as friends. I felt myself getting a moist eye and decided to finish the booklet later, in the privacy of our holiday cottage. When I looked at my new wife, tears were streaming down her face.

How could a simple Second World War Nissen hut, converted with discarded material, affect us so much? I felt a connection with the men, reaching out to us from the past. They had put so much of themselves into the building that a part of them remained. If the Italians had arrived on Lamb Holm with apprehension then they had left behind an icon of hope and peace.

Catherine and I had not spoken during our entire time in the chapel. It wasn't until we had closed the door behind us and were gazing across to Scapa Flow that the silence was broken.

'I'm going to find out everything I can about the chapel and the men who built it,' I said, 'where they were from, their lives in the camp and the work they did. I need to understand what made them create such an incredible monument and how they managed to do it within the restrictions of a prisoner-of-war camp.'

Catherine held my hand and smiled encouragingly, great wisdom and common sense behind the look. I smiled back, enthusiastic and excited; no great wisdom nor common sense. I had absolutely no concept of the enormity of the quest. It was one that would absorb me almost totally for the next four years (and goes on to this day).

During this time, I would seek out elderly men to hear their stories of life as

POWs in Orkney, I would speak to the descendants of the key artists behind the chapel and those involved in running Camp 60. I would bombard them with question after question, until there was no more to ask or no answers left to give. During this extraordinary period, strangers would become our friends and we would discover the chapel's secrets, which had remained hidden for more than sixty years.

We started our research that very afternoon, beginning by purchasing some of what would end up as a small library of relevant books, newspaper cuttings, correspondence and archive material; James MacDonald's excellent *Churchill's Prisoners: The Italians in Orkney 1942–1944* and Alastair and Anne Cormack's *Bolsters Blocks Barriers*. The latter provides a comprehensive story, in pictures, of the creation of the famous Churchill Barriers. We soon discovered that apart from the booklet published by the chapel preservation committee, the story behind the building's creation had never been told other than in newspaper or magazine articles, which, by their nature, provided only basic facts.

The next morning it was raining, so we made what was to be the first of many trips to the library in Kirkwall, sitting in the quiet of the reference section going through binder after binder from the archives, brought to us by the ever helpful staff.

'I bet you never imagined you'd be doing this on your honeymoon,' I whispered.

We had gone through numerous newspaper cuttings, correspondence and odd snippets of information and I was sitting, intrigued by a photograph showing Italian POWs with circles of cloth on their uniforms, when Catherine broke the silence.

'Look at this!' she said in hushed excitement, sliding a note across the table, handwritten in pencil.*

Dear Miss,
I am obliged to write you for telling you my feelings towards you. Since first time I saw you; I feel something in myself that is very difficult explain it tell you but it is not

* *Orkney Archive (OA): OA Ref D31/27/4*

[3]

possible because I do not know it. You understand the reason for these few word that I write to you. You do not know how great my love for you. Our eyes understand how much deep our love. My heart would never be tired to sing this loving hymmm but, I must close because I can't write long how you know – I am waiting a your reply, and if you please I beg you a your writing clear easy. With all my love.
Tony.

By the time I had read this, Catherine had found a typed sheet, explaining the story behind the mysterious letter from the lovesick Italian. It had been written in 1944, by which stage the Italians were a familiar sight in the streets and shops of Orkney's main town. One Italian from Camp 60 was a frequent visitor to J. M. Stevenson, which sold a variety of items. He rarely bought anything, but often stayed after his friends had gone, hanging around near the door.

One day he went in by himself and hurriedly handed over a sheet of paper to the girl who worked at the counter, before rushing out again without speaking. The girl was so taken aback that she gave the letter to the shop manager to read. It was the manager, Ernest Marwick, who had typed up the letter, copying it exactly, and adding the explanation of what had happened. We sat with the sheets of paper in front of us and read them again.

Catherine and I looked at each other, both with the same idea. We repacked the paperwork quickly, thanked the staff and twenty minutes later had found J. M. Stevenson. The sign had lost some of its letters but the shop was still there, tucked away at the end of Bridge Street.

'Come on,' I said. 'We've got to go in.'

We stood at the back, just as 'Tony' had done more than sixty years earlier, and tried to imagine what it would have been like all that time ago. Of course, it was completely different, but we felt another connection. It struck me then, as we watched shoppers buying their newspapers, that this is what the chapel is about; connecting people . . . those from the past, those of varying beliefs and religions, people with different nationalities and languages. It had helped to make enemies into friends and now it was reaching out to us.

1
HMS Royal Oak

The story of the chapel on Lamb Holm doesn't begin with hundreds of weary Italian POWs arriving in Orkney at the beginning of 1942. It doesn't even start in June 1940, when Italy's Prime Minister, Benito Mussolini, took the country into the Second World War on the side of Germany. The story begins around 1.20 a.m. on the morning of Saturday, 14th October 1939, when three torpedoes tore into the side of *HMS Royal Oak* and 833 men lost their lives. This tragedy included 126 boy sailors, the largest single loss of boy sailors in the Navy's history. The war had been going for only six weeks.

The 29,000 ton *Royal Oak* was anchored in Scapa Flow, more than 120 square miles of sea encased by the Orkney islands: mainland Orkney to the north; Hoy to the west with its famous 'Old Man of Hoy' rock stack; Burray to the east; South Ronaldsay to the south-east and a host of tiny islands in between.

It has been a safe haven for mariners for as long as there have been men sailing the seas. For centuries ships have sheltered there to avoid violent weather, limped in for repairs after storms or battles at sea, or have gone there for supplies and rest. Sometimes they waited for other ships, or signed on local men, for Orkney has long provided sailors who have travelled around the world.

In the First World War, Scapa Flow, with its easy access to the North Sea to the east and the Atlantic to the west, provided the obvious choice as a harbour for the British Grand Fleet. It was chosen again by the Royal Navy at the outbreak of the Second World War for the same reasons. To prevent attack from the sea a series of booms, anti-submarine nets and sunken 'blockships' —

old vessels well beyond their usefulness — were placed in the channels between the islands. They were designed to make Scapa Flow a secure resting place for the British Home Fleet.

But there was a flaw in the defences, which had been identified by Germany during a reconnaissance flight a few months earlier. There appeared to be a gap between the obstacles that were meant to have sealed Kirk Sound, the eastern entrance between mainland Orkney and the small island of Lamb Holm. If one of Germany's deadly U-Boats could penetrate Scapa Flow via that route, the devastation it could cause would be a terrible blow to Britain and the Royal Navy.

Could such a daring task be achieved? A plan was devised by Admiral Dönitz, who was then in overall charge of Germany's U-boats. He gave the task to one of his most experienced commanders, a man called Günther Prien. On 8th October, U-Boat U47 made its way from Keil without being detected, the mission so secret that even the crew were not told where they were going until well out at sea. When Prien told the men, he apparently added that anyone who didn't want to continue could leave the vessel. No one accepted his offer.

The night of Friday, 13th October was chosen because of the anticipated tidal and weather conditions, and earlier that day U47 lay on the seabed a short distance from Orkney. Timing was vital. Prien was relying on a particular high tide to be able to manoeuvre the vessel through the obstacles in Kirk Sound. Even with this advantage, the depth of water would give Prien very little clearance. The U-Boat's helmsman steered west into Holm Sound.

Prien's journey, *Royal Oak*, the Churchill Barriers and the Italian Chapel are connected by so many threads, many of which continue to this day. The local chapel preservation committee consists of a small group of Orcadians, who are dedicated to preserving the building and its contents. One of the committee is Alfie Flett, whose father Alfred was chief warden of the local civil defence during 1939. He and his wife Marion now live in St Mary's, which looks across Kirk Sound towards the small pier on Lamb Holm. Alfie recalled the following:

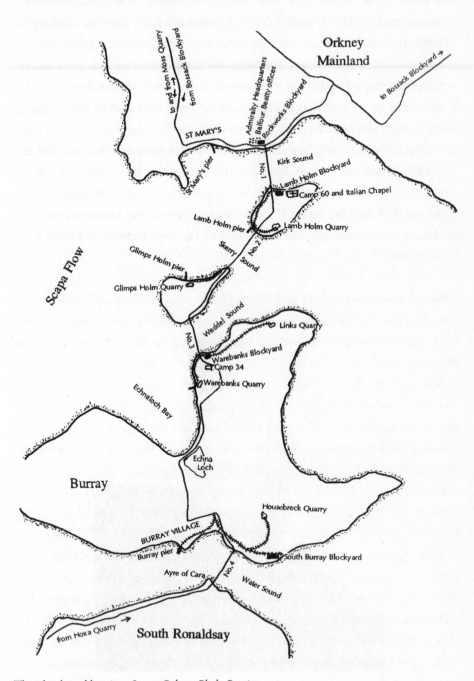

The islands and barriers. *Source: Bolsters Blocks Barriers.*

On the night that the *Royal Oak* was sunk, my father had returned home after a routine patrol, but he received a telephone call from the Kirkwall ARP (Air Raid Precautions) headquarters, asking him to check out a report that German planes were believed to have been dropping mines in the local waters. He duly set off. A short while earlier U47 had been forced to submerge for a period of time, to avoid being detected by a ship that had passed close by to its position.

My father was able to calculate from information later obtained that if the U-Boat had kept to Prien's original timescale he would have been standing on the shore only a hundred yards from where U47 would have passed. He couldn't possibly have missed it at such a distance. But the delay meant he was already on his way home when the U-Boat made its way through Kirk Sound.

Unaware of each other, U47 and Alfred Flett continued their separate journeys. But the U-Boat faced other hurdles, and for a while it was grounded, stuck next to one of the blockships that it was trying to pass. The crew endured some desperate moments but eventually the vessel was free and continued its passage unhindered into the harbour for the British Home Fleet.

Prien's journey into and out of Scapa Flow is a legend that has spawned numerous books, magazine and newspaper articles, not to mention many theories and much speculation about what actually happened that night . . . it was dark or lit by the northern lights, depending upon whose account you read. The events that followed were to result in Prien being fêted by Hitler himself and ensured that his name continues to be talked about decades later.

What is known is that U47 succeeded in entering Scapa Flow. As fate would have it, the vast array of warships that had been anchored in the harbour only days earlier had left. But there was one, whose heavy armament was providing additional anti-aircraft cover.

The *Royal Oak* lay at the north-east end of Scapa Flow and Prien soon saw it, along with another ship not far behind. At a distance of approximately 3,300 yards the U-Boat fired a salvo of three torpedoes, only one of which appears to

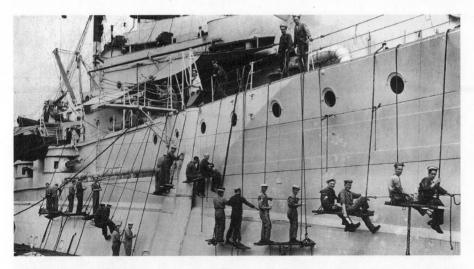

Painting *HMS Royal Oak*. How many of these men would go down with the ship on that fateful night in October 1939? *Source: Orkney Library Archives.*

have exploded. On board the ship, men heard a muffled explosion but the reply most received, if they asked, was that there had been a minor internal explosion and they should get back in their bunks.

On U47 Prien gave the order to reload one stern tube and fire again. The instructions were carried out, but there was no indication that this fourth torpedo had exploded and there was no sign of activity or alarm on the British ships. The U-Boat moved in closer and lined up to fire on the larger of the two ships from its bow tubes. Three torpedoes hit the *Royal Oak* in quick succession, and the ship sank in about thirteen minutes with enormous loss of life out of the complement of around 1,220. U47 slipped quickly out of Scapa Flow the way it had entered and headed for a hero's welcome.

The next morning, Margaret Omand looked out of her South Ronaldsay cottage, which was on the edge of Scapa Flow, and commented without realising the awful truth, 'the bonnie boat has gone today.' She would often sit with her young granddaughter Margaret and watch the nearby booms as they were moved to let ships pass. Years later, Margaret's father Thomas would play an important part in the chapel's survival. More threads . . . more connections.

The blockships *Lycia* (right) *Ilsenstein* and *Emerald Wings* were positioned between Lamb Holm and Glimps Holm in 1940 in an attempt to further block Skerry Sound. The *Ilsenstein* later provided tiles for the chancel floor in the chapel. *Source: Orkney Library Archives.*

Although his fame lived on, Günther Prien, who was decorated for his success with the Knight's Cross, did not get to enjoy it for long. His U-Boat went missing on 7th March 1941 while attacking a convoy off Iceland. By this time, some of the crew who had been involved in the sinking of the *Royal Oak* had changed vessels. U47's leading torpedo mechanic on the night of its entry into Scapa Flow was Herbert Herrmann. In 1944, the U-Boat he was serving on ran aground near Land's End and he spent the remainder of the war in British POW camps.

Alfie Flett's story continues:

One day in June 1989, I was at the Commodore Hotel in St Mary's when two men walked in. We got talking. One man was Herbert

Herrmann and the other was Taffy Davies, a survivor from the *Royal Oak*. The two former enemies had got to know each other after the war. My father was staying at my sister's house not far away, so I rang and asked her to bring him straightaway to the hotel. He introduced himself and told them his story, about how he was standing by the shore only moments before the U-Boat went past. It was an incredible feeling to see the three of them sitting together talking. I took a picture, which I still treasure.

While a POW and working on a farm in Dumfriesshire, Herbert Herrmann met a Scottish girl called Ina. After the war they married and he remained in Scotland for the rest of his life. He met survivors of the *Royal Oak* on several occasions and, in 1971, took part with some of them in a wreath-laying ceremony to remember those who died on that fateful night in October, 1939.

The destruction of the *Royal Oak* was such an extraordinary, daring exploit that a few days later Winston Churchill, at that point First Lord of the Admiralty, made a statement in the House of Commons in which he said:

It is still a matter of conjecture how the U-Boat penetrated the defences of the harbour. When we consider that during the whole course of the last war this anchorage was found to be immune from such attacks on account of the obstacles imposed by the currents and net barrages, the entry by a U-Boat must be considered as a remarkable exploit of professional skill and daring.

The nation was shocked by such a tragedy. One of the most unfortunate twists of fate is that another old ship was due to be sunk in Kirk Sound only a few days after U47 entered Scapa Flow. This additional obstruction might have prevented the U-boat's success, but we will never know.

A court of enquiry was held quickly to find out how the U-Boat could have entered the harbour. Until this was ascertained, and Scapa Flow could be more securely sealed, the fleet was kept at other destinations around the British Isles. Alternatively, ships simply stayed out at sea.

Churchill soon visited Orkney to see for himself where it was suspected the U-Boat had broken into the sanctuary of the harbour. He was accompanied by Sir Arthur Whitaker, Civil Engineer in Chief to the Admiralty, and asked him whether the eastern entrances, the 'sounds' between mainland Orkney, Lamb Holm, Glimps Holm, Burray and South Ronaldsay, could be closed completely. Whatever doubts Sir Arthur may have had, he answered 'yes' and so the greatest engineering feat of the Second World War began.

A team of experts from various fields was assembled and a hydrographic survey of the channels was carried out by *HMS Franklin*. The results from this enabled a scaled-down model of the eastern sounds to be built at Manchester University under the guidance of Professor Arnold H. Gibson. If given more time, a model of the whole of Scapa Flow would have been created, but time was short and everything and everyone was being pushed for speed.

Pieces of wood coated in paraffin wax were used to make replicas of the islands. Tiny blockships were made out of lead. A series of pumps and pipes were put together to simulate the alternating flow of the tide, and there was even a machine that produced the occasional 'storm'.

The hurdles facing the engineers were colossal. The combination of tides, the width and depth of the channels and the formation of the seabed and surrounding rocks, meant that many conventional methods of creating barriers could not be used.

Professor Jack Allen of Aberdeen University was brought in to conduct experiments to find the likely outcome of dropping large quantities of stone and concrete into the sea from overhead cableways. Trials included dropping miniature concrete blocks into a cattle trough along a 'causeway' in order to calculate the size, number and position of blocks that would be required. It is assumed that other measures were put in place to ensure the cattle did not go thirsty during this period!

Balfour Beatty was awarded the contract to build the barriers. The company was already operating in Orkney on several defence projects and its impressive pedigree of heavy civil engineering work included a recently finished 1,600-foot irrigation barrage across the River Tigris, at Kut-El-Amara in Iraq. The cableways used on this were considered suitable for the work to be carried out in Orkney. However, they would have to be transported to Britain.

During the winter of 1939, a phenomenal level of activity took place to prepare the groundwork for the project; suitable plant and equipment was sourced from around the UK and America, while the Ordnance Survey's geological department began examining potential areas in Orkney where quarries could be started in order to obtain stone.

Six sites were identified, three on Burray, plus one each on Glimps Holm, Lamb Holm and mainland Orkney. It was estimated that the project would require vast amounts of materials, time, men and money (the initial figure was around £2m, i.e., £67m in today's terms). All of these items were, of course, in short supply.

The owner of Lamb Holm, Orkney County Vice Convenor Patrick Sutherland Graeme, could not possibly have imagined how the ninety-five-acre island was about to be changed. Its solitude and peace would be taken away for ever, but in return it would acquire a fame that no one could have believed in those early months of the war, when everyone was focused on how to produce great barriers.

Apart from grass, nettles and gorse, there was nothing on Lamb Holm; no buildings, trees, animals or people. There was not even any water. However, its strategic position meant that the island was destined to play a vital part in the plan to prevent any vessel ever entering Scapa Flow again from the east.

Orkney was at the frontline of early hostile activities during the Second World War, with Scapa Flow an obvious target and the scene of many air raids. What is believed to be the first German bomb to land on British soil fell on to a field at Ore Farm in Hoy, resulting in potatoes falling from the sky on to a neighbour's house.

The first civilian to be killed on British soil by a German bomb died in March 1940 in Stenness, which is about ten miles west of Kirkwall. The planes flew on, passing near to the home of Patrick Sutherland Graeme, Graemeshall, on the south coast of mainland Orkney. On 16th March, his daughter Alison wrote in her diary:

Directly after dinner at about 8 p.m. we heard the drone of German

Patrick Sutherland Graeme was
Lord Lieutenant of Orkney
between 1948 and 1958.

Graemeshall, the home of Patrick Sutherland Graeme, who owned Lamb Holm and helped to save the chapel.

planes. Shortly afterwards guns opened fire. I went to the top attic and saw that the firing was coming from the direction of Scapa Flow. About five minutes later I went to my window and saw a plane, presumably German for it carried no lights.

I then looked out of the laundry window and saw a row of very bright flares towards the direction of New Holland. These were incendiary bombs. We watched searchlights and heard the drone of Hun planes now very near, then came a terrific explosion, which blew us out of the room. We rushed to the night nursery and took Elspeth and Sheena* down to the library. Soon after the firing got less.

There were two bomb craters in the drive the next day and the dining room, drawing room and spare room windows had all been blown in. Alison continued:

On the way to the village we were stopped by soldiers and told to keep well to the left as there was another crater in the road. At the Holm post office Mr Flett, the head warden, told us he had seen a plane machine-gunning the blockships. About twenty bombs were dropped all within 300 yards of the house, of which two were in the drive and two in the weed heap. Our cold frames were completely destroyed. The Shetland pony's foot was cut by a piece of shrapnel and several hens were killed, also a sheep. The kitchen door was blown in, a lucky escape for Cook and Cathie who were standing outside at the time.

Orkney became the refuge for survivors of merchant ships, trawlers and other vessels. There were many deaths in the local waters and bodies washed up on the shore were a grim reality of the horrors of war. More than one mass communal burial had to take place.

Local people became used to seeing military personnel going about the streets and as the population on the islands, normally around 20,000, rose to about

* *Patrick Sutherland Graeme's grandchildren by his eldest daughter Betty*

60,000, many buildings were commandeered for military use, with virtually all Kirkwall hotels taken over.

In May 1940, Scapa Flow saw the arrival of a ship different from the ones it was more used to sheltering. The *SS Almanzora* was a 16,000-ton Royal Mail liner that had been converted into an enormous floating warehouse. The list of items it contained was staggering: building material, excavators and drilling plant, explosives, pumps, railway track, sleepers, locomotives and wagons, generators and cables, food, fuel, huts, spare parts. There was even a small fleet of barges, which would be used to transport materials between the islands.

In the wider world, the news towards the end of that month was dominated by much more dramatic events at sea, with the evacuation of hundreds of thousands of Allied troops from the French beaches of Dunkirk.

The *Almanzora* also carried about 230 construction workers plus twenty admiralty staff. The first men to arrive on Lamb Holm rowed ashore from a Royal Navy drifter, jumping into the water to pull their dinghies the last few feet out of the sea. They had nothing more than muscle power and a few basic tools with which to prize loose and move stone slabs in order to build a pier, which was needed before anything larger could be brought on to the island.

To them, it must have seemed that they had been sent to the end of the earth, with some gangs living initially on the island in tents, returning to the ship only when necessary. The living conditions on the *Almanzora*, which was stocked with sufficient provisions for about 1,000 people for six months, were actually very favourable.

However, after only a few weeks, several workers demanded to be returned south, the work and weather proving too severe. This was a blow to the project, but at least those who stayed were keen to get on with the job and some remained until the completion of the barriers in 1944. Replacements were found for those who left, some coming from neutral Ireland where men were not subject to conscription into the armed services.

With much sweat and swearing, a stone pier was built and bigger items could be transferred from the *Almanzora*. (The ship was apparently rechristened the 'Almanrock' by locals because it stayed exactly where it was anchored until leaving in the November of that year.) Materials could now be brought ashore to allow the construction of camps for the workers, which were completed by

September. This task alone required a significant amount of manpower, with accommodation, water supplies, cooking, sewage, electricity, washing facilities etc. all having to be in place before the camps were habitable.

While this work was going on, the foundations for the cableways were started and blasting began at the sites of the proposed quarries. Work started on the construction of the block-making yards, which would eventually produce five- and ten-ton concrete blocks.

Trains had never been seen, or heard, in Orkney before, but as the months went by around ten miles of track were laid in varying gauges for the fifty-eight locomotives — a mixture of diesel, petrol and steam — and 260 wagons. They were used mainly to transport cured blocks from the block-making yards, loose rock from the quarries, or skips containing their stone-filled bolsters to the start of the barriers.

The trains were only part of a colossal amount of operational equipment, which included twenty-four cranes, sixteen crushers, nineteen excavators, fifty-one lorries and twelve dumper trucks. The floating plant consisted of seven barges, two steam tugs, two steam drifters, a diesel tanker and four launches.

To begin building the barriers, a system of 'end-tipping' was employed. The process involved lorries reversing slowly to the site of the barrier and simply tipping loose stones into the water. This was repeated constantly, day after day, over quite a period of time, with the vehicles eventually able to move further out into the sea by driving on the stones that had risen up from the seabed. However, it was a dangerous manoeuvre and more than one lorry followed its load into the water, never to be seen again, although it appears that the drivers always managed to get away safely.

The process ran into numerous problems, including the discovery that the red stone from the Glimps Holm quarry was disintegrating in the water, large patches of the sea around the start of barrier number two turning red as a result. This particular quarry was abandoned. End-tipping was only intended as a starting point and never as a method of completing the barriers. Apart from anything else, reducing the width of the channels made the tidal surge even fiercer. At speeds which reached twelve knots, it was already one of the fastest tidal races in the world.

If the project had been to construct a barrier across a river, where the current flowed in one direction only, the task would have been completely different. But the changing tidal flow gave barely twenty minutes of slack water and sometimes not even that. There are reports of the tide flowing at about four knots, and five minutes later flowing at a similar speed in the opposite direction. The constantly alternating direction of the water was only one of many unusual and significant problems presented to Balfour Beatty.

The landscape of Lamb Holm was changed even further when the first of the huge cableways arrived. Italy's entry into the war in June 1940 meant that they had taken a much longer route from Iraq than would otherwise have been the case.

Once back in Britain, the four electric cableways were strengthened by the Aberdeen crane manufacturer John M. Henderson Ltd as they were destined for a use for which they had not been designed. A steam-driven version, used to construct the Dornie Ferry Bridge in Ross-shire, was also brought to Orkney.

They were nicknamed 'Blondins' after the nineteenth-century French acrobat Jean-Francois Blondin, famous for such feats as walking a tightrope blindfolded across the gorge below the Niagara Falls, pushing a wheelbarrow, and even carrying his manager on his back! Everything about them was on a large scale and certainly nothing like the cableways had ever been seen in Orkney.

Once the 200-foot masts had been erected and embedded into hundreds of tons of concrete, the main carrying cable had to be fitted — it was eight inches in diameter and weighed around twenty-two tons. The seabed was too rugged to pull the cables between the islands so, to begin the process, a light steel cable was fixed to one mast. When the tide was at its weakest, a motor launch took the other end to the opposite mast.

This was then used to pull a thicker cable across the sounds, which in turn pulled over an even stronger one, until the main cable was in place. It was a process fraught with risks but eventually the masts were connected between each of the channels — Water, Weddell and Skerry — with two masts side by side across Kirk Sound, which was the deepest at more than fifty feet.

So the months rolled by, men fought with the elements, lorries continued to tip their loads into the sea and the Blondins were erected; the first one going into operation in June 1941 between Glimps Holm and Burray. Equipment, weather and sea fought a constant battle of strength. Plant and machinery were scarce commodities and any loss was greatly felt. Even boats were lost in the fast-flowing waters.

One day, the drifter *Token* got into trouble and was swept through Skerry Sound, sticking fast on some extremely dangerous rocks. The crew were saved by the bravery of the skipper of a small open launch called the *Kaki*. Within a couple of days there was nothing left of the *Token*. This wasn't the only boat to be destroyed during the early months and, tragically, several lives were also lost during the building of the Churchill Barriers.

One of the worst accidents occurred during September 1941 when eight men decided to use the skip on the cableway across Kirk Sound as a means of travelling from Lamb Holm to mainland Orkney. During the journey, the skip hit the water and all of the occupants were thrown into the sea with three subsequently drowning.

There were some serious injuries as well. During the summer, when one of the riggers was helping to erect a mast, his arm became trapped when a wire rope slipped out of its pulley. He was ninety feet in the air. Rigger Norman Rae and labourer Patrick Devery climbed up the mast immediately, the latter never having been up one before.

The two men managed to ease the injured man's weight off his arm by tying a rope around his waist. Four others ascended the mast and were able to take the strain on the wire rope so that Norman Rae could release the arm. He used a muffler as a tourniquet on the profusely bleeding limb.

Between them they got the man to the ground but his arm was so badly injured that it had to be amputated that same day. Norman Rae and Patrick Devery received a Special Command Mention by Sir Hugh Binney, Vice Admiral commanding the Orkneys and Shetlands. As fate would have it, Norman Rae was one of the men who drowned in the September tragedy.

Finding suitable labour continued to be a problem. Scapa Flow was such a highly sensitive military base that it had become the UK's first 'Protected Area' during the Second World War and this entailed restricted movement between Orkney and other destinations. The security services were already nervous about having large numbers of men from Ireland in the vicinity and an anti-

British slogan, discovered in one of the workers' huts, resulted in them being taken off the project.

Other men continued to be conscripted as the pace of the war increased. Even with special inducements such as paid leave and a one pound weekly hardship bonus, as well as the Ministry for Labour introducing a compulsory six-month period of work on the barriers, the project began to run short of manpower.

2
The Italians Arrive

While suitable labour to work on the Churchill Barriers was in desperately short supply locally, the British army held tens of thousands of Italians in POW camps across North Africa and, as more were captured, they were running out of camps in which to house them. The solution to the Orkney problem seemed obvious, although the practicalities of moving a large number of men over such a distance were hardly straightforward.

However, during the summer of 1941, more than 1,000 Italians were chosen from a camp in Egypt. They were selected individually, not just for their range of abilities and skills but also to eliminate those with strong fascist beliefs. One of the last things the British Government wanted was to have men, fiercely loyal to Mussolini, on the doorstep of Scapa Flow. So the Italians were vetted about their opinions of the war. As it turned out, a few fascists slipped through the net, but not many.

In the months that followed, when tens of thousands of Italian POWs were transferred to camps throughout the UK, and it was not possible to interview individual men in any detailed way, a significant percentage of the POWs who landed on British soil remained loyal to Mussolini. This was later to give the government some interesting challenges, but the early group destined for Orkney were, on the whole, just happy to be out of the fighting.

Amongst the many men chosen was a small, quiet man, whose life before being called up had consisted largely of painting religious statues, frescoes at local churches and traditional iconography. He was called Domenico Chiocchetti and would later play a key role in the creation of Orkney's famous chapel. By 1941, Domenico was thirty-one years old. His daughter Letizia was one of the first people to be contacted during the writing of *The Italian Chapel* and gave an insight into her father's character:

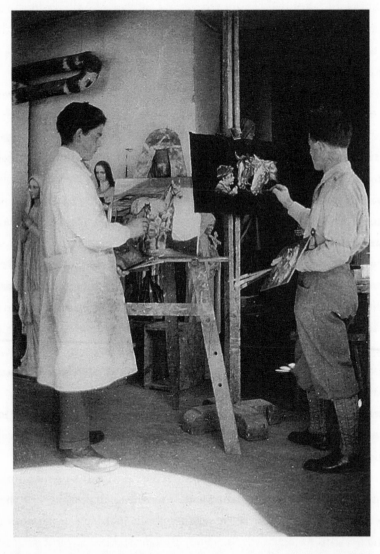

Chiocchetti (right) learning his craft in Ortisei, near Bolzano, during the late 1920s.

He had always wanted to be an artist, but he was the youngest of twelve children in a peasant family and there was no money to send him to art school. It was only when he was fifteen years old that he had the opportunity to go to Ortisei in Gardena Valley, which is world famous for its craftsmen and wood carvers. He worked as an apprentice for two years in a studio and later as a painter for five years.

While doing this he learnt the secrets of the painter's trade. He also attended evening classes in decoration and drawing. As he loved art deeply, he observed the various artistic expressions, particularly the frescoes of the local churches and also traditional iconography.

He used to come back to Moena in the summer to help his relatives in their little boarding house. Public transport was not very developed at the time and the journey from Ortisei could take all day, so Dad very often used to take a shortcut across fields and two mountain passes, walking for four or five hours.

In 1931, he did his national service in the Sixth Anti-Aircraft Regiment in the town of Mantova. His training lasted only six months, instead of the usual eighteen. He then came back home, but was recalled several times on different occasions, sometimes for only fifteen days. In June 1939, the general feeling of an imminent outbreak of war was very strong amongst people. So even Dad was called up and sent to Mantova.

They embarked at Naples and travelled to Bengasi, Tobruk and finally Bardia. For six months they stayed behind the lines doing military exercises; his duties were mostly done in an office as a copier and expert graphic drawer. He recalled that he was sent for a whole week into the desert, alone with a telescope and a compass, to notify the flight paths of airplanes over the telephone. He later used to smile, saying he never fired a shot throughout the whole war!

In his own words, in an article published in the *Orkney Herald* in 1959, Domenico explained how he was captured:*

* *OA Ref 31/27/4*

In June 1939, I was in Laste, a village in the province of Belluno, working on the decoration of a church. From there I was called up and sent to the Sixth Anti-Aircraft Regiment of the Mantova Division destined for Libya. After six months at the front I was taken prisoner by the Canadians* and was sent to a camp at Geneifa in Egypt. In the camp we were all hungry, but luckily I was not there for long.

There was a request for artists amongst the prisoners and I came forward. I was taken to the English headquarters where I was put to work on copying and enlarging family photographs. To me, it seemed a paradise, where I was well fed by an excellent Indian cook. I stayed there for five months and was paid with Egyptian piastres, which I used to spend on food for my famished companions in the camp. I made more than a thousand copies while I was there plus some portraits from life. In October 1941, my camp was to be transferred to India but, thanks to a Scottish corporal, I was instead included in the contingent destined for England.

Domenico never met the Scottish corporal again and without that last-minute decision to include him, Orkney would probably not have its little Italian chapel today. A chapel may still have been built in Camp 60; many were created around the world by Italian POWs during the Second World War, but most were taken down along with the other huts when camps were disbanded in later years.

At the time of writing, Coriolano 'Gino' Caprara is in his early nineties. He spent his captivity in Camp 34 on the Orkney island of Burray, so was not involved in the construction of the Lamb Holm chapel. However, his phenomenal memory for detail provides an invaluable insight into life in the POW camps and work on the barriers. The following is his account of an incident that occurred shortly after his capture by the British army in January 1941:

We had been forced to march for miles in the desert until we arrived, tired to death, at Sollum, where we embarked on a cargo ship to be transferred

---

* Chiocchetti was confused by the large hats worn by the soldiers. He was actually captured by the Australians.

to Alexandria. Thousands of us were stowed below in the hold of the ship.

We were already in a bad state and after a couple of hours had to endure the stench created by so many men, who were compelled to vomit, shit and piss where they stood. Consequently, it happened that a man felt sick and passed out. After a while he was lifted up and taken to the upper deck. This is the premise of what a friend of mine and myself planned during the voyage. Both of us agreed to simulate passing out, falling on to the dirty floor. So we did. Shortly we were taken and transferred to the upper deck where we could have the benefit of fresh air.

But after about one hour we were noticed by an officer who ordered us to return down to 'hell'. My friend said that we should 'pass out' again, but I said the guard would recognise us and detect our trick. So we decided to wait until the relief of the guard and when we saw he was a new man we decided to simulate a new faint.

Like before, we were brought up to the open air again. As it was getting dark, my friend and I, instead of lying on the deck, slipped away behind a big ship's anchor where no one could see us and we had the opportunity to spend all night in the good air. Frankly, we felt sorry for the others but in these difficult situations we adopted the old saying, 'All is fair in love and war.'

If any of the Italians thought life was going to be easier in Britain, their journey to this new land perhaps gave them some idea of what lay ahead. Packed on to a goods train, they were taken to Port Said where they boarded a cargo ship that set off south, through the Red Sea.

The ship called at various ports such as Durban, Cape Town and Freetown, to restock with supplies, arriving finally at Liverpool on 10th January. (The previous month virtually all work on the barriers had stopped in order for the construction workers to erect two POW camps in Orkney in preparation for the arrival of the enemy.) Gino Caprara recalls:

We were at sea for almost three months and it was not easy for us because we had been held below in the hold of the ship. We all had been suffering from seasickness, not to speak of the fear of being torpedoed and sunk by a German submarine. However, thanks to God, we arrived safely and were happy to be on dry land again.

One doesn't have to imagine for long what it must have been like to be kept below decks for almost three months to appreciate that Gino's comment, 'it was not easy for us', is something of an understatement.

From Liverpool, the Italians were taken by train to Edinburgh where they stayed for several weeks in a disused building that had been a home for the deaf. They underwent medical checks and further registration formalities and were issued with chocolate-coloured uniforms that incorporated three red circles, one on the back of the jacket and the outside of the left arm, and the third on the front of the right trouser leg.

These were target discs, designed to make it easier for British guards to shoot someone who they considered was trying to escape. The uniforms had holes in the material underneath the circles to prevent the cloth from being removed and the uniforms worn in an escape attempt. It was not a great beginning.

The brief spell in Edinburgh gave the men the opportunity to write home. Sending and receiving letters from Italy had proved to be extremely difficult while based, or moving around, in camps in North Africa. Certainly, for the last few months, while they had been on the ship, it had not been possible at all. Letizia gives an example of her grandmother's fears at not hearing from Domenico for a long period of time:

For months, while he was in Libya, his family didn't get any news from him. His mother, plainly worried, sickened seriously and, only when my father arrived in Scotland and managed to let her have a letter via the Red Cross did she quickly recover!

The Italians were transferred to Orkney during the beginning of 1942. There are conflicting accounts about when they arrived, with most articles saying this was during January, although Gino Caprara and ex-POW Bruno Volpi (Camp 60) both say they arrived at their respective camps on 23rd February.

One article even suggests all of the men arrived at the Burray Camp and that later on roughly half were sent to Lamb Holm, but this would imply that Camp 34 could accommodate around double the number it was intended for, which seems unlikely.

Whatever the timings, the POWs departed from Aberdeen docks and sailed, with a destroyer as an escort, to what would be their home for the next two-and-a-half years. Although the journey was just around the corner compared to the distance they had travelled from Africa, the prospect of being herded below decks into cramped and airless conditions once again must have filled them with dread, with the old fear of being torpedoed gripping many a heart.

However, they arrived without mishap. The shock they faced is impossible for us to appreciate today. They were used to golden days of sun and for most of the last eighteen months they had been in the North African desert.

Burray was at least large enough to be inhabited, whereas the buildings on Lamb Holm consisted only of what had been put up since the arrival of the *Almanzora*. Everything had to be brought to the island. Drinking water came from mainland Orkney via a pipe that had been fixed to the top of an anti-submarine net.

Camp 60 consisted of thirteen Nissen huts, enclosed within a barbed-wire fence. Nissen huts were a common sight during the Second World War because they could be transported in sections, erected quickly and were relatively cheap. Their inventor, a Canadian engineer called Peter Nissen, could hardly have believed the fame that the buildings named after him would later achieve, although few people remember them affectionately. The inner and outer 'skins' of corrugated iron sheets, fixed to a frame of iron and wood, meant that the huts were cold in winter, hot in summer and noisy when it rained.

However, the building could be assembled easily on site, and the classic barrel shape provided greater protection against bomb blasts than square-sided structures. The Nissen huts needed to be fixed to a concrete base and the ones in Camp 60 were fastened down with additional steel stays to prevent them from being blown away.

The huts had bunk beds down each side, sufficient for around fifty men per building so there was not a lot of space. On top of every straw-filled mattress were four blankets, a towel, soap and shaving blades, one spoon, one fork and two metal dishes. Heat for the entire hut came from a pot-bellied black stove that sat in the middle of the building.

The Italians were given an allocation of coal for each day but there was little wood as trees were scarce in Orkney. Those with beds at the far ends gained little benefit from the stove, particularly the poor souls near the door. Domenico later said of his arrival at the camp:

> The little island could hardly have appeared more desolate: bare, foggy, exposed to the wind and heavy rain. The camp consisted of thirteen dark, empty huts and mud. Here I had the misfortune to be separated from my friend Pennisi, who was sent to another island. There were no other painters and so we were divided up one to a camp.

Once they had claimed their bed, the Italians went to explore their new home, such as it was. Local man Andrew Petrie was helping to repair some of the huts in Camp 60 on the day the Italians arrived. In a documentary about the chapel made by Jam Jar Films in 1992, he explained what happened:

> We built Nissen huts for them but it began to snow and they were simply flooded. The huts were only thin corrugated iron and the wind had twisted them. We couldn't really fix them up tight. I was working on caulking the seams. The Italians went into the huts, threw down their gear and within a few minutes some of them came out and started to talk to us while we were working above the door, telling us about their bambinos and asking us about our bambinos as well!

The largest building was the mess hall, which contained huge kitchen ranges. There was also a canteen, where men could get hot drinks and purchase items such as toiletries and writing paper. Just outside the camp was a small but forbidding looking concrete building . . . the punishment block.

If the men looked north, they would see the south shore of mainland Orkney, a distance of around 2,000 feet, while to the south was the tiny island of Glimps Holm. This was uninhabited even during this period of frantic activity to construct the barriers, although men worked on Glimps Holm during daylight hours. To the east was Holm Sound and then the North Sea.

It was to the west, and Scapa Flow, that men would often later stare with stunned astonishment at the great armadas before them . . . destroyers, battleships, cruisers, dreadnoughts. The ships would be waiting, sometimes to provide protection to conveys, at other times for news of the whereabouts of the German fleet.

The British officer in charge of the two Orkney POW camps was Major Yates, who had to split his time, and his presence, between both sites. Not an easy task, which was made even more difficult when travel between the islands entailed a boat trip.

The men in Camp 60 lined up for their first roll-call and a British officer walked up and down. They didn't realise that they would stand on that windy parade ground and be counted many hundreds of times before they were to leave. They were told they had to help build barriers . . . to hold back the sea.

Several photographs were taken of Camp 60 work groups. The man standing on the far right is Palumbi, who would later make the beautiful rood screen in the chapel. *Photograph by James W. Sinclair.*

What they thought of such a concept can only be guessed at, but even many local people considered the project flawed and that the current between the islands would simply wash away any material dropped into the water.

Before the men could be sent to work they had to be fitted out with an assortment of outdoor clothing, such as oilskins, boots and thick gloves. About thirty men were chosen to remain in the camp and not to work on the barriers at all. This included Domenico, who was given a job in the administration office, copying documents. His daughter recalled:

> My father always said he had been rather lucky. Being part of the staff he didn't have to work on the barriers at the mercy of the bad weather, but worked mainly indoors. At the beginning his duties basically were painting and designing posters, sceneries for the little theatre or various decorations that were needed around the camp, as well as helping to keep it clean.
>
> Men on staff lived in a smaller hut, which could accommodate only fifteen instead of more than fifty. He said life in the camp was miserable but honourable. Even the food was poor but enough for everyone.

There was a lot of competition for a job in the kitchen, which held the big attraction of warmth. The cooks were considered to have full-time jobs. A separate group was given cleaning and maintenance tasks and included men such as the camp barber, tailor and shoemaker, who were also expected to provide these services to their fellow prisoners.

Dressed in their heavy overalls and oilskins, the Italians eventually set off to their various destinations. The POWs were allocated into groups of about forty, which were then marched away, escorted by an armed guard and one of their own NCOs (a non-commissioned officer, i.e. an Italian corporal or sergeant). As they marched away that morning, there were shouts of 'Viva il Duce!' from a few who felt loyal to Mussolini or those who simply wanted to display their anger and frustration.

Most of them were sent to work in the Lamb Holm quarry, the block-making yard or the island end of the cableway that was linked to mainland Orkney or the one that was linked to Glimps Holm. Other regular jobs included repairing the railway track, which ran near to the shore in places and was often damaged during storms.

The most strenuous work took place in the quarry and the Italians must have looked on in despair at the confusion that met them. More than one man might well have thought he was looking at a scene from Dante's *Inferno*, as mechanical diggers fought a duel of strength with the rock face, trying to prize away slabs that the latter did not want to give up.

Around the quarry, lorries full of stones whined with the effort it took to drive away, replaced quickly by empty vehicles, eager to be filled, like the hungry gulls that circled overhead. The men were split into smaller groups. Their task, like that of the diggers, was to fill the lorries with stones. They heaved rocks that the diggers could not reach until their arms and backs cried out for rest, and while their hands and faces were stung by the icy winds they sweated underneath their heavy outdoor clothing, which restricted their movements.

In 2004, while at home in Gloucester watching a programme about Orkney, eighty-five-year-old Guido DeBonis was astonished to discover that the chapel on Lamb Holm still existed. He had been a POW in Camp 60 and, in 2008, made an emotional return journey with his family, sixty-four years after he had left the island. Most of the ex-POWs who have since returned to Lamb Holm had assumed the building was taken down after the war and many found out only by chance, often decades later, that it was still standing.

The return visit by Guido DeBonis attracted significant local publicity, as well as from leading Scottish newspapers. Shortly afterwards, he started to provide information about his time in Camp 60, and so began another fascinating period of correspondence:

I was captured in Egypt in 1940 along with the rest of my platoon and ended up in Pretoria, working alongside African woman in the fields. I loved Africa and wanted to return in later life. However, by 1942 I had been transported to Orkney . . . and snow! I had never been so cold in my life. I had been sent to Camp 60 to work on the Churchill Barriers.

We rose at 6 a.m., sometimes earlier if the weather was good. Then we had breakfast and went to work, either on lorries or sometimes marching, depending upon which job we were on that day. The work was hard . . . making the blocks for the barriers . . . and our hands became cracked, sore and sometimes bled.

Crushing plant near Housebreak quarry on Burray. *Source: Balfour Beatty.*

As they rested at midday, eating the welcome soup and bread that had been sent over from Camp 60's kitchen, the quarry took on a totally different feel in its quietness, as if suddenly the anger had gone. Like the Italians, the Balfour Beatty workers also stopped to eat and huddled in small groups with their sandwiches and mugs of tea, trying to shelter from the wind. Everyone began to cool down quickly and as the lorry took the empty soup containers and dirty bowls back to the camp, the quarry was once more filled with noise, dust and rage.

Lorries carrying stones either went to the Lamb Holm block-making yard, where the rocks were crushed to make aggregate for concrete, or they were sent to unload their cargo into bolsters. These were steel wire nets, which the Italians made by bending large wire sheets, approximately 17 x 6 feet in size, around a metal frame called the 'former'.

Two end panels were added and the sheets fixed together with spiral rods, which created the basic shape of the cage. The whole lot was dropped into a skip, after which the top 'wings' were folded back and the 'former' removed, leaving the steel wire basket ready for its load of stones. Once filled, the top was closed and sealed with a steel rod to ensure the contents were contained.

The Balfour Beatty construction workers had been dropping these bolsters again and again into the sea, where they disappeared beneath the surface with a great splash, never to be seen again. Now it was the turn of the Italians to watch the results of their sweat and toil disappear under the sea.

Life on Lamb Holm hit the Italians hard; the work was strenuous, the weather cruel and the conditions in the camp grim. They had to endure walking in deep mud every time they went out of the door, whether they were going to eat, see someone in another hut or even to visit the latrines during the night. There was always mud to negotiate. Trying to keep the cold at bay proved difficult and the men were only allowed to keep the stove going all day on a Sunday, their one day off work.

They lay in their beds at night, exhausted but often unable to sleep because of the rain beating noisily on the metal roof, like the sound of machine gun fire, wondering how they could possibly have ended up in such a strange and hostile place. The food was also alien to them. As POWs, they were given similar rations to the British army, so were actually better fed than many civilians in the UK, but it was a point that was perhaps not appreciated at the time.

'Our breakfast was porridge, with salt, and at lunchtime while working we were brought bread and soup by the guards,' said Guido. 'It was transported in lorries. Evening meals were soup, bread, cheese and sometimes pasta. Later into the war we went to local farms and bought eggs.'

None of the guards spoke any Italian and those Italians who spoke some English were often confused by the strong accents of men who had come from as far away as Liverpool, Tyneside and London. This resulted in regular misunderstandings and some bad feeling.

'The guards were very strict,' said Guido. 'Some would be unkind but mostly they were okay. If you got into trouble you were locked up, but still taken to work in the daytime.'

No one wanted to be on this small Orkney island, including the soldiers guarding them. It was all heading one way . . . STRIKE! Going on strike is never something to be entered into lightly, but to take this action as POWs showed just how desperate the Italians had become and after about one month they rebelled. The leaders of both camps, elected by the men upon arrival, made an official complaint to Major Yates.

Their first point was that by being made to construct barriers to seal the harbour for the British Home Fleet, they were involved in 'works of a war-like nature', while their position so close to Scapa Flow placed them in danger. Both facts contravened the Geneva Convention. The POWs demanded they were moved to different camps, otherwise they would refuse to work.

The threat resulted in frantic calls to the War Office in London, which led to the Inspector of POW camps making the long journey to Orkney. Meetings were held and the camp leaders were informed that, according to the Geneva Convention, they were subject to the same regulations as those in place for the armed forces of the detaining power.

The Swiss Government provided the role of 'Protecting Power' for Italian POWs under British control and the men in Camp 60 were told that their complaints would be passed on to this relevant body, which was based in London. In the meantime, the men should all go back to work. They flatly refused and were subsequently put on a fortnight of 'punishment rations', which consisted of only bread and water for three days with standard meals served every fourth day. The Italians were more miserable than ever.

After more than sixty-five years, it has been impossible to piece together exactly the sequence of events surrounding this incident. Soon after this initial strike had begun, it appears that the two camps were split and a new commandant was brought in for Camp 60, with Major Yates continuing to be in charge of Camp 34.

Gino Caprara explained what happened on Burray:

I consider it important to explain our point of view about the work we were commanded to do. For us Italian soldiers it was war work and, appealing to the Geneva Convention we went on strike and refused to do that kind of work. Another discomfort was added to our strained circumstances as we were punished and our food was only bread and water.

After about twenty days of these conditions and stress, an International

Red Cross Committee came over and told us that the construction of the barriers was not war work but had been planned long before to provide facilities to the inhabitants for their transport to and from the mainland. I don't know how many of us believed what we had been told but notwithstanding our deep convictions, we decided to set to work after all.

However, I am pleased to say that after that the relations with the British commandant and his staff become better. The Italian POWs carried on their jobs seriously and productively even if the job itself and living conditions were not easy. Many of us fell ill with psychological problems, some due to homesickness, some due to the hardness of the work and some to the difficulty of getting used to the different weather conditions.

On Lamb Holm, Guido DeBonis was caught up in the Camp 60 strike.

When the strike happened we complained that the work was too heavy and stopped working. We were sent back to camp, locked in and our food was stopped. After two or three days we realised that if we didn't work we would not get fed so we went back to work. The British were not too bad about the strike, probably because they knew we would not want to go without food for long. They joked with us about it.

Further meetings took place, including one to which the local Provost of Kirkwall was invited in order to give a civilian view of the situation. This was when it was put to the men that the 'barriers' were actually 'causeways' that had been planned for some time but never built because of a lack of manpower and money. Once completed, they would enable the population of Burray and South Ronaldsay to travel to mainland Orkney by road instead of relying on boats, which were always at the mercy of the weather.

The project officially became one to build *causeways* and, from then on, the authorities were careful not to use the word 'barrier'. Work on the 'causeways' continued although there were some notable incidents of rebellion, including an

The Warebanks blockmaking and storage yard on Burray.
Source: Balfour Beatty.

escape attempt and the refusal of the occupants of one hut in Camp 60 to get out of bed one morning.

The men had endured a particularly long period of harsh weather and one day, faced with rain yet again, the men in one hut simply stayed where they were, apart from going for meals or to the wash block. The British left them alone until that night, when soldiers burst in and made the Italians stand outside while they conducted a search.

They were let back in when nothing was found but the POWs were hardly warm in their beds when the guards came in again and made them stand outside while another 'search' was carried out. This went on throughout the night. In Orkney it is so often the weather, not men, that determines a course of action.

The following morning was dry and bright. The Italians in the hut got up, had breakfast and went to work like everyone else. Each side had made its point and the British made no more of the incident.

With the nearest land to Lamb Holm also being an island, the possibility of escape was extremely remote. However, despite this and the dangers posed by the sea, an escape attempt was made.

Orkney man Harry Russell had joined the Royal Navy at sixteen as an HO (hostilities only) volunteer, which meant he would automatically be demobbed after the war. It was not long after the POWs had arrived that he received an order to search Scapa Flow for three Italians who were believed to have escaped from Camp 60.

'We were called out to search for these men and when we found them they were pretty glad to be picked up,' said Harry. He continued the story:

Without being detected, they had managed to make a small raft out of empty oil barrels and a few wooden hatches from a blockship. Fortunately for them they launched the craft on the west side of Lamb Holm, into Scapa Flow, because if they had gone into the North Sea they would probably never have been seen again.

We found them fairly quickly and they were sitting shivering, with their hands up, saying 'I surrender'. They had a huge tin of bully beef, although nothing on them to open it, and a replica of a Sten gun made out of steel piping and wood. We found it later, tucked in between the barrels. It was quite a good imitation. We pulled them on board and gave them a mug of tea before taking them to the mainland for questioning. I never found out what their intentions were. Later on, they were simply returned to the camp.

3
Summer, Strife and Strikes

Although strikes in Camp 60 continued to flare up, the Italians settled into a routine of sorts, albeit an arduous one. Reveille was at 6 a.m. and men would have to make their beds, clean huts and prepare for ablutions by 6.35 a.m., when roll-call was taken. This was followed by shaving, ablutions and hut inspection. At 7 a.m. they would fall in on the parade ground for fatigues, followed by breakfast at 8 a.m., after which they would get ready for work. The men returned during the late afternoon and would have some spare time before supper.

Once men had left the mess hall after breakfast, the cooks would clear up and begin making soup and bread. The kitchen was fitted out with a well-equipped bakery and, fortunately, one of the Italians had been a baker before being called up.

'One thing I remember is the fact that we always had fresh bread,' said Guido.

While the camp was empty, the 'cleaning and maintenance' men would ensure that everything was ready for the return of their colleagues. This would include making sure there was sufficient coal by the side of the stoves for that evening.

The Italians obtained permission to build concrete paths between the huts so they no longer had to walk in mud while moving around the camp and, with the arrival of spring, better weather and longer daylight, the conditions improved further. The British introduced a quota system and when the specified tasks were completed for that day, they were allowed free time. The Balfour Beatty

A painting by Chiocchetti showing the Italians working on the barrier across Kirk Sound.

personnel had to complete their full shifts no matter how much work they had done.

In 1995, during a celebration to mark the fiftieth anniversary of the official opening of the Churchill Barriers, a speech was given by Alistair Wivell, managing director of Balfour Beatty Construction Ltd, whose father had been the general foreman for the building of the barriers from 1940–1944. He gave an interesting insight into the decision to change the working conditions of the Italians:

> As you might expect, there are many stories of incidents which illustrate the differences in temperament between Scots and Italians. One which my father was involved in was the problem of lack of production in the blockyard at Lamb Holm, which was manned almost entirely by POWs. It was noted that most of the group were keen woodcarvers and model-makers and eventually it was agreed to give the POWs more time for their hobbies by reducing their eight-hour shift in return for increased production.

In no time, production was up by over forty per cent, for a one-and-a-half hour reduction in shift! Naturally everybody was very happy! As a further concession, the POWs were unofficially allowed access to the blockships to remove wood panelling and metalwork, including the fire bars from the ships' boilers, which were later used for some of the wrought-ironwork in the chapel.

The authorities recognised the danger of bored soldiers and a recreation hut was put up in the camp. The Italians were given some more concrete and they made the first of what would eventually be three billiard tables. They fixed a blanket to the top and carefully smoothed the surface with razor blades before adding rolled-up blankets to form cushions along the sides. They made concrete balls, although proper billiard balls were later obtained from Kirkwall.

'In a very short time the prisoners had transformed Camp 60 into a garden with flower beds and cement paths,' said Domenico years later. 'In the mess hut we built a little theatre and I designed and painted the scenery for every production. I did the decorations for the recreation hut, including caricatures of the English sergeant who was nicknamed "Wooden Leg" and who was very popular with us.'

The Italians could easily keep up-to-date with developments in Europe, as they were allowed to have a radio in the mess hall and could listen to this whenever they were free. There were also two regular newsletters — *Il Corriere del Prigioniero* and *Il Corriere del Sabato* — printed in London by the British Government for the tens of thousands of Italian POWs in the country.

But in many other ways the men on Lamb Holm were isolated. No communication was officially allowed with the POWs in Camp 34 and apart from the Orkney men employed by Balfour Beatty, the Italians had little contact with local people. Opportunities to visit Graemeshall, just across Kirk Sound, were grabbed at. More than once, a small group from Camp 60 would make their way, under armed escort, to obtain plants for the newly dug borders around the huts.

Contact with nearby families meant a huge amount to the Italians. Many of them had left children behind when they were called up and they worried and fretted about them constantly. Most had not seen their own wives, sons and

A billiard table made out of leftover cement. Eventually, there were three in the Camp 60 recreation hut. *Source: Orkney Library Archives. Photograph by James W. Sinclair.*

daughters for more than two years and men feared that small children would forget them. While at Graemeshall they often met Patrick Sutherland Graeme's daughter Alison, who lived there, and sometimes Elspeth and Sheena.

The most delightful encounter whilst researching for *The Italian Chapel* was to meet the 101-year-old Alison. For many years her sister Betty lived a few doors away in the same Kirkwall nursing home, until her death in August 2009 at the age of 105.

John Muir is an old friend of the family and, as secretary of the Italian Chapel Preservation Committee since the 1960s, has been a contact point for people around the world with an interest in the chapel. He provided help and contact details throughout the book's research and arranged a visit to Alison.

Dressed elegantly, she was someone whose face was alight with curiosity . . . and a huge welcoming smile.

'Now tell me everything that you are up to,' said Alison, who had already been briefed about the reason for the visit.

'Oh yes, Major Buckland was a very nice man and so was the Italian sergeant major,' she said. 'He made a little wooden toy for my niece Sheena, which consisted of a wooden board with a row of ducks on top. A weight hung below on a string and when this was moved the ducks bobbed up and down. The Italians made lots of toys for the local children . . .'

Alison pointed to a large box in the corner of the room. It was full of her diaries, which she had kept since being a young girl.

'I used to keep five-year diaries but when I reached ninety I only bought one-year versions,' she said. 'I stopped when I got to ninety-five . . . there was nothing more for me to say.

'I have some pictures from the Second World War. They're in my book. It tells my whole life story and was compiled by my niece for my one hundredth birthday.'

The book represented a huge amount of effort and presented a fascinating account of her life; photographs of her as a (very attractive) young woman, stories and pictures of Alison and the chapel, a large photograph with the Queen Mother standing outside Graemeshall.

'As we were waiting to have our picture taken, the Queen Mother asked me how I managed to keep my hair tidy in the strong Orkney wind!' said Alison with glee.

Amongst the original men to arrive in Camp 34 was Father Luigi Borsarelli. With the priest's help, artist Sergeant Giovanni Pennisi gathered a team of craftsmen and began building a chapel, just as his good friend Domenico would do many months later. Pennisi was later to play an important part in the creation of the Camp 60 chapel. Gino Caprara has fond memories of the priest:

Our chaplain was a very special man. He spent most of his spare time giving lessons to illiterate men so that they could learn to read and write while in captivity. I myself am indebted to him because it is thanks to him that I am still able to correspond in English after more than sixty years.

He was a very good teacher and, generously, in 1942 he lent me ten pounds to buy books on grammar etc. Once I returned home I wrote to him and said, 'Father, I owe you ten pounds.' He said that I had already extinguished my debt by my excellent English.

Life in the camps improved, as the Italians altered their surroundings and the winter storms receded into the distance. During the summer of 1942, while the men in Camp 34 were building a chapel, Domenico created the first of his works of art. He was given permission to obtain a quantity of cement and barbed wire. As well as being a painter, he was also a gifted sculptor and had the idea of creating a statue for the centre of the parade ground.

He began by making a framework out of wire, working in the late afternoon or during the evenings when others were resting, writing home or playing cards. Day after day he wrestled to turn a material designed for war into something that represented peace. Eventually, he had the shape he desired and his trained artist's eye could see what could be achieved with it, although to anyone else it probably looked like a hopeless tangle.

Domenico began to cover the armature with cement, applying the wet soggy mass again and again, moulding and sculpting as it dried, forcing his will upon it. This went on for many weeks, while his comrades watched with a growing sense of wonder and respect.

'My first undertaking there was the making of a statue of St George on horseback with the dragon at his feet,' said Domenico. 'I made it from concrete, and it was over three feet high. I used barbed wire which was got for me by the prisoners who were working on the dyke.'

When the statue was complete, the men built a concrete base to put it on and positioned it in the centre of the parade ground. Considering the materials Domenico was working with, the final result is extremely impressive. St George, mounted upon a rearing horse, thrusts his spear into the head of the dragon at the horse's feet. It is a moment of drama, movement and triumph. The statue did indeed become a focal point of the parade ground, a point around which men would gather. Bruno Volpi said years later: 'It is a concrete representation of the desire to eliminate all evil, all wars that cause pain and injustice to so many people. It is the symbol of a will to "kill" all misunderstandings among people of different cultures.'

There is a story that while the statue was being built, Bruno Volpi, who was a good friend of Domenico, had written the names of every Italian POW in Camp 60 on several sheets of paper. These had apparently been put into a container along with some Italian coins and placed in the centre of the plinth, directly beneath the dragon. When the statue was placed on to the base, the list was sealed forever.

Wanting to know if the story was true and whether the list of names still existed required the help of local artist Gary Gibson, who had been the art teacher at Kirkwall Grammar School for many years before retiring in 1990, by which time he was assistant headmaster. He had supervised much of the restoration work, which had also included, unfortunately, having to repair the statue following some severe vandalism in the early 1970s.

Was the story about the list under the dragon true and, if so, was it still there? 'Yes and no,' answered Gary, who went on to explain what had happened.

Italian POWs gathered around Chiocchetti's statue on the Camp 60 parade ground to celebrate its completion. *Source: Orkney Library Archives. Photograph by James W. Sinclair.*

It was nearly forty years ago now. People woke up one morning to find that the previous night vandals had badly damaged Domenico Chiocchetti's statue, to the extent that the broken statue was lying on the ground. I offered to try to repair the whole structure and a local building contractor, whom the committee had hired, delivered it to my garage, which I used at that time as my workshop.

The original armature consisted of old barbed wire and the damage done had created a jigsaw of broken parts, so I inserted reinforcement rods at various points to strengthen the whole statue before I reassembled it. The lance had rusted too much to reuse, so a replica was made by a local blacksmith.

With the statue removed, it was possible to look into the concrete base. Near the top was an old-fashioned milk bottle and when I lifted this out I could see it contained the remains of several sheets of rolled-up paper along with some Italian paper money and coins. But over the years water had entered the bottle.

The sheets had been decorated script, but only remnants of flower decoration at the corners survived. These I dried. The paper money survived intact. I replaced all of this in a sealed plastic container and included two British coins from that year.

When the statue was completed the contractor did not want to handle it, so as I was an officer in the Territorial Army I got the local Lovat Scouts Infantry of the 51st Highland Volunteers to help me replace it, using muscle power in place of hydraulics.

His skill and dedication means that no one looking at the statue today would realise just how badly damaged it had been. However, it was a disappointment to learn that the list was destroyed as it meant that the chance to find out the names of the Italians who had been in the camp was lost. There was no other known list that existed.

It was not many months after the POWs arrived at Camp 60 when Domenico was sent to the punishment block situated just outside the perimeter fence. He had been sent to 'Kalabush', as the Italians said. Domenico was a quiet, kindly man but he also liked to make people laugh and in an interview for the Jam Jar Films documentary he told the story of the gull:

> A very funny memory is the story of the seagull. One day some friends and I captured the seagull with some bread on a fish hook. Once captured, we brought it to the camp. I painted one wing red and the other one green, leaving the rest white.
>
> Then we let it go and when the gull flew away it looked just like an airplane and we shouted 'Italian airplane'. But the commander saw us and punished us. He put us in jail for two or three days on bread and water and that was it. The commander was really angry.

Although the POWs were often exhausted from their day's work, spare time had to be filled and an assortment of groups emerged. The stage at the end of the mess hall was in regular use between the two theatre groups that had been formed, one made up of men from the rural areas in the south of Italy and the other from the more urban parts of the north.

There was a large cultural difference between the two groups and this showed itself in the type of plays that were performed. Those from the north preferred works such as marionette productions from Venice, while the southerners stuck to playwrights from their part of the country whom they knew and understood. Domenico ran the northerners' group and was often called upon to paint the backdrops.

However, frustration and resentment at their situation were often just below the surface. Water was a valuable commodity and one day the authorities noticed that there was unusually high usage, with levels dropping more than they would expect. Upon investigation by the guards it was discovered that the taps in the wash block had all been left on.

The soldiers turned them off, only for them to be all turned on again later. Spring-loaded taps were fitted to the sinks, but the culprits tied these down with whatever came to hand. It then became a regular event for guards to inspect the wash blocks and remove the string etc. that was holding down the taps. It did nothing to help relations between the two sides.

Domenico played mandolin in the camp band, which grew in size and

The stage for a performance in the mess hall of Camp 34. *Source: Orkney Library Archives. Photograph by James W. Sinclair.*

stature. A small selection of instruments was available in the camp canteen, while some men made their own and a few were donated by local families. Music was an important part of camp life and there were often performances on Sunday evenings in the mess hall. With the seemingly never-ending supply of concrete, the Italians built a bowling alley, complete with concrete bowling balls.

Men took up hobbies such as sketching and many of them began to make a variety of objects, some of which are treasured items in Orkney homes and museums today: intricately carved boxes; ashtrays adorned with Spitfires and Hurricanes; and a cigarette lighter that looks like the Eiffel Tower. There is even an accurate model of Milan Cathedral, made out of matchsticks.

The POWs tried to sell what they made to the guards or construction workers. Strictly speaking, they were not meant to be given money and so they usually traded in cigarettes, which was the most common currency in the camp. Like many military servicemen of the time, a large number of the Italians smoked. As POWs they were given a weekly allowance of thirty-five cigarettes a week. If this wasn't sufficient, men would slit the thick RAF issue cigarettes with a razorblade to make the tobacco go further.

Like POW camps the world over, the inhabitants of Camp 60 created a still to produce alcohol. The guards left them to it and it was a common sight for tubs of fermenting liquid to be plopping away quietly amongst the warmth of the huge kitchen range. A tea urn had been converted into the still, which despatched, at a painfully slow speed, clear amber liquid that was stored with great reverence in an assortment of glass bottles.

During the summer, the British had to get used to other new visitors — American GIs — who had started arriving in the country at the beginning of the year. 'Over paid, over sexed and over here', as the well known phrase went. The bombing of British and German cities intensified.

In North Africa, the fierce fighting between Montgomery's Desert Rats and Rommel's Afrika Korps continued and a huge counter-offensive by the Germans resulted in the capture of the Libyan port of Tobruk in June. Thousands of Allied soldiers were taken prisoner. Tobruk was the very place in which many of the Italians in Camp 60 had been captured the previous year.

When their time was not spent working or playing games, men sat or lay on their bunks, talking and smoking. But once the lights were out, the men on Lamb Holm fretted not about global issues, but that parents would no longer be alive by the time they eventually returned to Italy, or that brothers and friends might have been killed in action. They lay, tormented by the suffering and danger facing wives and children, for much of Italy at this time was a battleground. Years after the war, Bruno Volpi said:

> In a POW camp, life can be a dull daily routine, not always improved by billiards, table tennis, football or amateur theatre; all things that we POWs had the strength to keep going. That wasn't enough, not for most of us at least.

Helping to overcome some of the frustrations of camp life; a boxing match in Camp 34.
Source: Orkney Library Archives. Photograph by James W. Sinclair.

Nights were our worst enemy. Long nights when thoughts went back home to those we loved. Bad news from home, that somehow reached us, was a cause of deep depression that no entertainment could ease. Only in thinking of something nobler, more elevated, could we find inner peace and hope. So the tiny chapel came gradually into existence.

Friends would try to help those who had been overwhelmed by despair, but there was not much to be cheerful about and there was little that Gerbino Rocco, Camp 60's doctor, could do. He was allocated the end of one hut as his infirmary, but was given virtually nothing in the way of equipment or medication.

'Unless someone was feverish or injured they were expected to work and the usual treatment was *aspirina!*' said Gino referring to Camp 34.

What they most needed was not a physical cure but something more noble . . . something spiritual. However, Camp 60 had no priest or chapel and although some men gathered in the mess hall to pray on a Sunday, they felt the lack of a proper place of worship very strongly. In a way it was like the weather, the food and the lifestyles — it chafed against everything they knew and understood; everything Italian.

One of two weekly newspapers produced by the British Government for Italian POWs held in Britain during the Second World War. *Source: Churchill's Prisoners.*

The Red Cross parcels arriving at the camp contained mainly books. Some POWs tried to learn English but many picked up what they knew from conversations with civilian workers, which often resulted in a mixture of words with little understanding of grammar. The parcels from Italy generally provided a variety of small treats such as chocolate or cigarettes. Woollen gloves and socks were often included but the most treasured items were letters and photographs of family and friends. 'We could write home twice a week,' said Gino.

At first we were supplied with a card where we could write only a few words, greetings and signature. Then we received a special sheet of paper consisting only of twenty lines. We could not write news about the war, where the camp was, or news that could be involved with politics etc. Our address was: name, surname, camp number, UK. The sheet could be folded into three sections, fastened by a little flap without sealing it. There was no envelope.

Censorship of mail to and from Orkney was extremely strict. This was not only because of the close proximity of Scapa Flow but also because the British Government feared that Germany, which occupied Norway, could use Orkney as a way of invading Britain. Around 100 people were employed in Inverness with the sole purpose of reading Orkney mail. Any remarks in letters that were considered potentially dangerous, but were thought to have been written innocently, were cut out with scissors, whereas letters containing comments that appeared more sinister would be passed on to a higher level for further investigation.

Work on the causeways continued, six days a week, with hundreds upon hundreds of bolsters being tipped from skips, disappearing into the sea, never to be seen again. Many on the project began to lose heart at the apparent lack of success and it was decided that for a while, in two channels, bolsters would be dropped in the same spot instead of along the whole line of the cableway.

The six blockyards produced a total of around 300 five-ton blocks a day. Moulds into which concrete has been poured can be seen in the foreground of the picture, with empty moulds waiting to be filled by the crane. This photograph is of the blockyard at South Burray.
Source: Balfour Beatty.

After a relatively short period of this concentrated dropping, a great cheer went up one day when the top of a wire basket, complete with its load of stones, could be seen sticking above the water at low tide. It proved that the project was possible and there was a great sigh of relief in many quarters. The men went back to dropping bolsters along the entire length.

The varying widths and depths of the four sounds meant that the progress of each was different but, by the summer of 1942, the foundations in Weddell Sound, between Burray and Glimps Holm, had risen sufficiently to almost separate the sea.

The Italians in Orkney may have been out of the fighting but they faced dangers in the work they did and the death of one Italian is recorded following an accident. Geovanni Scarponi was one of the skilled workers. He was rushed to the Balfour hospital but died from his injury. Orcadian John Rosie explained what happened in the Jam Jar Film documentary:

> Unfortunately one of the Italians was killed. He was quite a good mechanic and was working on a compressor in the garage when he went to start it and it backfired. He was hit on the head with the handle. He was buried locally and the boys made a gravestone for him.

Another Italian POW died of pneumonia. Both men were buried with full military honours in St Olaf cemetery, about one mile from Kirkwall, a platoon of men being allowed to attend each service. After the war their bodies were exhumed and returned to Italy.

Throughout the summer of 1942, the Italians worked and worried, they played music and cards, they tended their little gardens and they prayed for an end to the war that had taken them so far from their families.

4

The Arrival of Major Buckland

Colonel Lynch, the POW Inspector of Camps, arrived in Orkney on Tuesday, 15th September 1942, in order to settle a series of strikes by POWs, which had rumbled on throughout the summer. In addition, accusations of slackness and neglect of duty had been made against the staff and guard of Camp 60.

When he had left London, Colonel Lynch had been under the impression that POWs in both Orkney camps were on strike, whereas only those in Camp 60 were involved. Camp 34 was still under the control of Major Yates. The officer was prevented from visiting Lamb Holm because of the weather, so reported to the headquarters of Orkney and Shetland Defence.

The following day, Colonel Lynch arrived on Lamb Holm and, after a brief tour of the camp and meetings with the commandant and his officers, he sent for the Italian camp leader, two sergeants and two corporals. He explained who he was and that he had arrived 'not to investigate alleged grievances, which they knew perfectly well had been dealt with, but to punish those still further as soldiers who refused to obey lawful commands'.

Later, he met again with the commandant and ordered that those POWs not going back to work by 18th September should be put on twenty-one days of No. 2 punishment diet, as laid down in the Rules for Military Prisons and Detention Barracks. Colonel Lynch provided a copy of this book on loan for guidance. He selected 18th September as the punishment commencement date so that POWs should have three clear days of normal diet since their last spell of No. 1 punishment diet, and so that they could have no legal grounds for a complaint on that score.

Colonel Lynch was given to understand that most of the POWs would return to work. Subsequently, he made an inspection of the British Lines and reported finding evidence of poor administration, including a dirty cookhouse and 'a member of the guard sitting on his bed in his own hut, some 300 yards from the guardhouse, smoking peacefully'. There was also 'a general atmosphere of slackness and ignorance of their duties on the part of the officers and men'.

He ordered that POW workers and non-workers should be segregated within the compound and was told that this could easily be carried out as there were posts and ample wire. Various discussions then took place both at Camp 60 and at the nearby headquarters.

On 17th September Colonel Lynch once again visited Camp 60 and during his meeting with the commandant told him that: 'I realised his task was not an easy one but that I was equally sure that the men were being intimidated by a group, which if we could discover we would eliminate.'

On arriving back at Lamb Holm on the Friday, Colonel Lynch discovered that 157 of the 403 POWs currently housed in Camp 60 were, at that point, on strike and locked up in huts guarded by provost staff armed with Tommy guns. One POW was under close arrest for throwing a stone at a sentry and would later be tried by Court Martial.

Colonel Lynch immediately gave various orders to the guards, which included segregating part of the camp with poles and barbed wire, a task that had not so far been done. He also made several recommendations to his superiors.

On 24th September, Major Buckland took over as the new camp commander of Camp 60. At the age of fifty-three he was rather a 'fatherly' figure to the Italians, most of whom were in their twenties or early thirties. He also loved everything to do with Italy and had the huge advantage of being able to speak some Italian. His arrival heralded a new phase in camp life.

Major Buckland's concern for the welfare of the Italians under his care and his subsequent enthusiasm for the creation of the chapel makes him a key figure in the 'Miracle of Camp 60', but there is little published information about him.

The starting point was John Muir, who emailed the address of the British

Seated right to left, Camp 60's deputy camp commander Major Booth, camp commander Major Buckland and Captain Miller. Standing are Lieutenants Burke and Thomson. *Source: Orkney Library Archives. Photograph by James W. Sinclair.*

officer's granddaughter, Fiona Zeyfert. She was able to give an insight into an important character involved in the events of so long ago.

Born in 1888, Thomas Pyres Buckland left school to become a printer's apprentice in Bangor, but he ran away to Liverpool and worked as a steward on board liners travelling between England and America. At one stage he was on the White Star Line ship *SS Cedric* and there is a story that the family thought he had been transferred to the *Titanic* just before its tragic maiden voyage. Certainly, his poor mother was frantic until he could get word to her that he was still on the *Cedric* and perfectly safe.

He was in the army during the First World War and was based for a while in Italy, which was where he picked up the Italian that would prove so useful many years later in Orkney, a destination he could hardly ever have imagined being sent to. His open manner appealed to the POWs under his care and he would often walk around the camp after roll-call, speaking to the men and listening to their fears. Domenico summed up his feelings about the British officer:

> During the first year there was some trouble in the camp but then the commandant was changed and in his place was Major (now Colonel) Buckland who was like a father to us prisoners. Everything in the camp went well under him, assisted by Sergeant Major Fornasier.

Although he was only twenty-six, Sergeant Major Guerrino Fornasier was the most senior Italian in Camp 60. Indeed, there were few Italian officers in Britain because they were exempt from manual work under the Geneva Convention. This meant the British Government had little use for them at home, where they were desperate for unskilled and skilled labourers.

Guerrino was born in Venice but his mother died when he was two so his father took him to Florence, where his own parents lived. As a young man, Guerrino had been in the *Carabinieri*, the Italian military police, and joined the army soon after war was declared.

Sergeant Major Fornasier was the main link between the British officers in

Guerrino Fornasier talking to an Italian farmer in Brescia at the start of the Second World War.

the camp and the POWs, passing orders in one direction and raising issues in the other. He appears to have been well liked and respected by all sides and, later, when they were no longer enemies, he became a good friend of Major Buckland.

As the year wore on, the men were forced to finish work earlier in the afternoon because of failing light. Anything that took them away from the howling winds on the barriers or moving stones in the quarry was welcome, but it meant they spent longer periods in their huts, which was not good for morale.

When gangs arrived back at camp they would first of all get rid of their heavy outdoor clothing and then go to the wash blocks to clean up. There was sometimes an afternoon roll-call on the parade ground and there were regular searches.

Men would generally rest on their bunks before supper, which was normally quite early in the evening. Since they had arrived at the beginning of the year, the cooks had tried to change the menu to suit Italian tastes, but attempts at making something resembling pasta had resulted in a few disastrous meals. However, the new commandant did his best to help secure the type of ingredients required and, on the whole, they considered their food adequate during wartime.

Certainly, the food available locally in Orkney was more plentiful than in many parts of England, so much so that Major Buckland would later send food parcels to his wife in Shropshire.

As Christmas approached, men missed their families more than ever. They pulled together to try and make the occasion as enjoyable as possible. Domenico made a crib, which was put on the front of the stage in the mess hall, and the cooks adjusted the rations during the weeks beforehand so that they could do something special over the few days of Christmas that the men were given as holiday.

But it was a grim time. In North Africa, the fortunes of war continued to swing back and forth and, towards the end of the year, Montgomery had once more gained the initiative. The news from Italy was not good and the men in Camp 60 worried. Despair was often just beneath the surface when a man was quiet and keeping to himself.

Sergeant Major Fornasier's daughter, Gina Ellis, said: 'My father often talked to the men in the evenings, while they were playing billiards or cards, and it

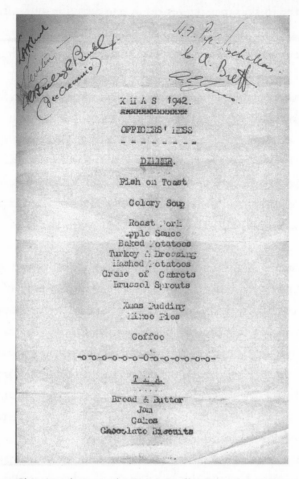

Christmas dinner in the Camp 60 officers' mess, 1942. The menu is signed by some of the officers.

was during these conversations when he learnt that a lot of them suffered from depression and loneliness.'

The approaching winter made them shiver with apprehension as much as the drop in temperature. Whether the experience of their first winter helped them prepare for this one, or made them more wary of it, is not known. Gino Caprara expressed his feelings in Camp 34:

From my own experience, our Christmases were not joyful. How could they be? Yes, we had extra food, special mass, even a hut and crib were built by our craftsmen and it was not a working day for us. But was it a Merry Christmas for our dear ones at home? I leave it to your honest sensibility.

And so 1942 turned into 1943 and the POWs completed their first year in the Orkney camps.

Orcadian Bill Johnstone ran the Lamb Holm power station, which had been built not far from the small stone pier. A huge amount of electricity was required to run the cableways, stone-crushing equipment, machinery at the block-making yard etc. and the power station operated two 323-kilowatt generators, believed at the time to be the north of Scotland's biggest diesel generators.

Bill Johnstone stayed in the island's Balfour Beatty camp during the week, but went home to mainland Orkney at weekends. One day, he was asked by some Italians if they could have some of the switch oil that was used with certain electrical equipment. He gave them a small quantity and a few days later they were back asking for more. This went on for a period of time and eventually, completely baffled as to why they wanted the oil, he asked them what they were using it for.

It transpired that the Italians missed not having something to grease their hair with and the pure oil was the nearest thing available! Before the Italians left Orkney, they presented him with a glass lemonade bottle containing a beautiful crucifix to thank him for his generosity.

Bill Johnstone's daughter, Rosemay, still has the bottle from the lemonade manufacturer R. Garden Ltd, although it is displayed at the Kirkwall museum during special events. Producing some POW Camp 60 tokens that had been kept as a memento, one with the name 'Pietro' on it, Rosemay recalled:

The man who gave my father the lemonade bottle was called Pietro. Pietro worked in the kitchen of the Balfour Beatty camp so he was well known by the civilians. Father got to know several of the Italians. He showed one man how to make a lobster creel, so that he could catch his own lobsters. I'm not sure if he ever caught any.

[61]

Rosemay revealed a selection of photographs, including one of her father in later life with his Rolls Royce, which was used many times to transport members of the Royal family when they visited Orkney. This included a trip to the Italian chapel by the Queen Mother in 1980. By this time, ill health had stopped Bill from driving the Rolls Royce himself and the driver on the day was his son, Reynold. However, Bill did get to meet the Queen Mother at the chapel.

By the spring of 1943, a 'knife-edge' of bolsters could be seen along the entire length of all four sounds at low tide and it was not long before this was raised sufficiently to be visible at high tide. This meant that the initial objective of closing the eastern entrances to Scapa Flow had been achieved, and no enemy vessel would be able to enter that way again.

With the waters no longer racing back and forth through the sounds, it was possible for divers to inspect what had been happening underneath the surface much more easily. One of the things they found was that many of the wire nets had distorted but this had resulted in the bolsters nestling and linking together, thus forming a more stable structure. Work commenced to widen the barriers.

During May 1943, the German and Italian forces in North Africa surrendered to the Allies. At the beginning of July, the Allies invaded Sicily and began what was to be a long, fierce and costly battle as they pushed the German army off the island then, over many months, gradually further north into Italy.

One of the Italians captured by the British in Sicily during those initial weeks of fighting was a man called Ugo Pizzi. At the time, he was far from being able to offer any resistance, being near to death's door. His son Alberto explained what happened:

My father was very ill . . . literally dying from malaria, but the 'enemy' took care of him. He always said that he owed them his life. He was later transported to the Orkney islands, were he stayed, except for a few months spent in Skipton before his return journey home.

Soon after he arrived on Lamb Holm, he found himself on a small

Ugo Pizzi in 1941 when he enlisted in Milan. The men were given a picture of themselves to send home to their families. He was seriously ill with malaria when taken prisoner by the Allies, after they invaded Sicily in July 1943. When he had recovered, Pizzi was sent to Camp 60.

beach. He walked along the sands to the sea in order to wash himself and found a stiff, cloth case that had been washed ashore. He used the case for the rest of his life to keep his shaving gear in.

He said that he worked hard on the barriers and 'did his job'. He was treated with respect and humanity and learnt a few sentences in English as well as some popular wartime songs such as 'Begin the Beguine', which we sometimes heard him sing in later life! We assume that the men sang these songs in the little shows they performed for the local people in Orkney.

My father got used to drinking tea with milk, something quite unusual in Italy, and many years afterwards my eldest daughter still remembers this strange habit of her grandfather.

But while Ugo Pizzi was lying feverish in Sicily and being cared for by the British, events were taking place in Italy that would subsequently affect him even when he was as far away as Camp 60. On 25th July, Italy's Grand Council of Fascism had a vote of no confidence in Mussolini and the next day, King Victor Emmanuel III replaced him as Prime Minister with Marshall Pietro Badoglio.

The following day, British newspapers were full of the story, with the headline in the *Daily Mirror* being typical: 'MUSSOLINI IS SACKED'. The newspaper went on to say that the king of Italy had assumed command of Italian forces. Mussolini had been in power for twenty-one years and his fall was announced by Rome radio at 11 p.m. the previous night. Italy's continuation on the side of Germany was now in doubt.

The news tore through the Orkney POW camps. Although some Italians considered it to be no more than British propaganda, there were many who believed it. But whatever viewpoint was taken, everyone was shocked and confused.

Gino gave an indication of the reaction in Camp 34:

At the news of Mussolini's dismissal in 1943 there was bewilderment and incredulity. Nobody could believe such a thing could happen and many of us feared that in Italy civil war could break out. Amongst us there were some faithful to fascism and, convinced of high treason, stupidly threatened every kind of revenge once we returned home.

Some of the Italians, including Chiocchetti, ended up in the punishment block just outside Camp 60 and their lives became even more strictly controlled, as shown by the regulations on the following page.

Standing Orders for Prisoners of War under Sentence of Detention

1. The strictest military discipline with silence will be maintained.

2. On entering your cell an NCC* will hand over to you your bedding, cell equipment etc. You are personally to check each article and to satisfy yourself that all articles are correct, i.e. that all blankets are whole, no furniture broken or damaged or windows broken, and that walls and doors are not defaced. Should you find any breakage or deficiency bring this to the notice of the Camp Commandant through the Provost Sergeant. Should any breakage or damage occur during your period of detention you will be held responsible for the payment or replacement or repair of same.

3. Communication by talking, signs, etc. is not allowed, neither is singing or whistling.

4. When speaking to or being addressed by members of the staff you will always stand to attention.

5. When shaving, all doors will be left wide open. No man is permitted to leave his room without permission of the Provost Sergeant or his representative.

6. After meals all plates, knives, forks and spoons will be placed on the floor outside the door.

7. To report sick or to make application to the Camp Commandant, apply to the Provost Sergeant or his representative at Reveille.

8. If you lose any article of clothing or equipment report the fact to the Provost Sergeant or his representative.

9. Beds will not be made down until the whistle is blown at 20:00 hours.

10. When your door is knocked after you are locked up, stand to attention in the centre of your room and answer 'All correct' or otherwise.

11. If a member of the staff enters your room stand to attention at the head of your bed.

12. When the whistle is blown stand to attention until you are told to 'Carry on'.

* Non-Combatant Corps

13. If you want to make a complaint, make it in the first place to the member of the Provost staff on duty. If you are still dissatisfied ask to see the Provost Sergeant. If you still think you have cause for complaint apply to see the Camp Commandant. It is only when you consider that the Commandant has failed to redress your grievance that you should complain to any visiting or inspecting officer. Pending any decision you will carry on with your normal work and duty.

14. No articles of any description may be put out of your window or into any ventilator etc. in your cell. All rubbish will be disposed of under instruction from the Provost staff.

15. Keep these orders clean. They will be complied with strictly.

16. Any man disobeying these orders will be reported.

5

Padre Giacomo

The man who was the catalyst for the chapel's creation was an Italian priest called Gioacchino Giacobazzi, although he was more commonly known to his flock as Padre Giacomo (many letters and documents refer to him as Father Giacobazzi and these have been left as written). It appeared initially that very little has ever been published about him.

Buried in the Orkney library archives was the translation of an article he wrote, which was published in *Il Corriere del Sabato* during the summer of 1944. In addition, in 1959, the *Orkney Herald* newspaper reproduced an article that Padre Giacomo wrote about his time in Orkney, after he had been contacted in Italy by the retired Colonel Buckland.*

A great deal of interest in the chapel was generated during 1959 following the 'discovery' of Domenico in Moena, who had been interviewed earlier that year for a radio programme broadcast by the BBC. Letters and correspondence between men who had been in Camp 60 were flying around during this period, the chapel once again bringing people together.

Padre Giacomo's account of events was excellent background material, but what had happened to him after he was repatriated in 1945 and where did he end up in his old age? The only leads were that he had been a Franciscan and that in 1959 he was living at the monastery of Stella Maris, Milano Marittima.

* *OA Ref 31/27/1*

Gioacchino Giacobazzi, November 1919. *Source: Padre Giacomo Giacobazzi Biography.*

Finding nothing on the Internet giving a lead in Italy, a website turned up for Craigmillar, a Franciscan order in Edinburgh. Father Antony Collins, who was listed as the guardian and parish priest, helped in the attempt to find out what had happened to the priest in the camp. He replied to an email the same day with the full address in Italy of the monastery he believed was the right one.

A letter to the monastery resulted, two months later, in the arrival of a copy of the biography of Padre Giacomo Giacobazzi, quite possibly the only one in the UK. Published in 1997, albeit in Italian, the book had been written by a man called Berardo Rossi and gave the full life story of the priest, complete with a wide selection of pictures.

The priest who was so involved in the creation of Orkney's famous chapel was born on 9th April 1895 in the little hamlet of Montorso, just outside Pavullo nel Frignano in the province of Modena. The second of eleven children born to Domenico Giacobazzi and Luigia Balestra, he was baptised Gioacchino.

The family lived in a farmhouse and Gioacchino learnt quickly to help with chores, including taking the sheep and cows out to pasture. At the age of five he began to help out at mass at the local church, and started to learn Latin.

In October 1901, he started school in Albareto, now a suburb of Modena, about an hour's walk away, but four years later the family moved to a small built-up area of Pavullo nel Frignano, and Domenico Giacobazzi, along with other men from the district, sailed to America in the hope of making more money. Gioacchino's mother was left in charge of the family.

Gioacchino, who was bright and keen to learn, soon reached an age where his future needed to be decided upon. The local priest was consulted and, in 1908, Gioacchino, along with several other local boys, left for Seraphic College, a Franciscan seminary in Bologna. They would all later become priests.

Life suddenly became very different for twelve-year-old Gioacchino. The college, which was modelled on a monastery, expected great discipline and enforced rules that would be common in a religious establishment. However, he flourished in the environment and at the age of sixteen became a novitiate at Santa Maria del Paradiso in Faenza.

Padre Giacomo Giacobazzi during the Italian-Ethiopian War of 1935–36. *Source: Padre Giacomo Giacobazzi Biography.*

Brother Giacomo (James) continued with his studies and calling and everything went well until the morning of 12th January 1915, when a piece of official looking correspondence arrived in the post, ordering him to prepare to join the army and enter the Great War to end all wars.

He reverted back to the name of Gioacchino and became a foot soldier, sent to fight at the front, where going around on all fours could save a man's life—one day in the trenches, a sliver from a grenade sheared through the visor of his cap. But Gioacchino's education and talents were soon noticed by his superiors and when it was discovered he could type he was sent to work in the offices of the General Staff.

He was promoted to corporal before being dismissed on 30th October 1919. He returned to Santa Maria del Paradiso in order to complete his studies in

Padre Giacomo. Photograph taken around 1955. *Source: Padre Giacomo Giacobazzi Biography.*

Possibly the last photograph taken of Padre Giacomo.
Source: Padre Giacomo Giacobazzi Biography.

preparation for the priesthood. He was ordained in 1921 and moved, shortly afterwards, to Santa Maria di Campagna in Piacenza. In 1930, he was sent as guardian of the Osservanza church in Cesena, where the monks were involved in caring for the local parish and school.

When free of his duties Padre Giacomo would cycle through the local mountains and pine forests, where he would often relax, pray and reflect in the peace. But peace, in every sense, was not to last and, in 1935, he was called up once more, this time as a military chaplain.

He was given the rank of Lieutenant and set sail from Naples on 1st August to an unknown destination. Once at sea, the ship set a course for East Africa. The men on board were to join the Italian-Ethiopian War. This time there was no question that he would be involved in fighting and he was sent to one of the many hospitals. He returned to Italy two years and two days after leaving and moved to the Chiesa dell'Osservanza in Bologna.

But war was on the horizon again all too soon and, in 1938, Padre Giacomo was sent back to Ethiopia. He was in Gondar in March 1941 when informed of the death of his father and was still there on 22nd May when the British surrounded the field hospital he was working in, taking him, and the rest of the Ialians in the camp, prisoner.

As the British were at the gates, the priest ordered a man to run and take down the Italian flag in order to save it from falling into enemy hands. The soldier brought back the flag just in time for Padre Giacomo to stuff it into the bottom of his satchel without being seen. He placed his personal effects on top. That flag would still be in his possession many months later, when his life was to take another completely unexpected turn . . . and he would arrive on a tiny Orkney island called Lamb Holm.

6
Capitulation

Two things happened in September 1943 that changed the lives of the Italians in Camp 60 completely. The first event was Italy's Capitulation, which the men heard announced on the radio in their mess hall. The second event occurred at the end of the month with much less fanfare, and concerned the arrival of Padre Giacomo on the small liberty boat at the Lamb Holm pier.

Later, both of these incidents were to play a vital role in the creation of the chapel, but building a place of worship was on no one's mind as the news of Italy's Capitulation went from hut to hut. The effect was dramatic and the result, momentary chaos. Everything had been turned around in an instant. Countries that Italy had been at war with were suddenly no longer enemies, while those that had been allies? Nobody quite knew what to think.

The front page of the *Daily Express* for 9th September carried a headline that echoed several other UK national newspapers that day. ITALY IS OUT: BERLIN CRIES 'TREACHERY'. The newspaper went on to explain how General Eisenhower had announced on radio that Italy had surrendered unconditionally. Berlin reacted with fury.

'Italy's Capitulation was a worrying time for us all . . . worried about our families back home,' said Guido DeBonis.

In the Orkney camps hopes were raised and dashed with every conversation. Surely they were not prisoners of war anymore? Surely Britain could not hold them against their will as it was now an ally? Surely this meant they were free and could perhaps go home?

'We hoped we could go home, but on that date Italy was still occupied by the Germans and we realised that our return would not be possible,' said Gino Caprara.

Throughout much of 1943, the Allies had been discussing what should happen if Italy was no longer an enemy. The British and American Governments were prepared to consider negotiating with the Italians with regard to their position (unlike Germany and Japan for whom unconditional surrender would be the only prelude to peace).

However, certain elements within the government in London felt that this was not a viable option. British military personnel had provided the main fighting force against the Italians and more than 70,000 British servicemen were, at that time, held in POW camps in Italy.

On 3rd September, the Italian armistice with the Allies was signed by General Castellano, on behalf of Badoglio. The announcement of the agreement by Eisenhower five days later caught the Badoglio Government off-guard. News of the switch of allegiance had not been communicated throughout Italy's armed forces and, as Germany rushed in extra troops, Badoglio, King Victor Emmanuel III and other military staff fled to Pescara, where they set up a government under Allied protection.

There was turmoil in Italy, with the army basically having no orders to follow. The situation left many unanswered questions about Italy's status as well as the position of around 500,000 Italian POWs, who had been captured by the Allies at different stages of the war and were held in various countries, including America.

The British Government walked an extremely difficult road as it tried to keep public opinion at home on its side, while not offending its Soviet partner and, at the same time, giving at least some concessions to the new Italian Government. Also, Britain was desperate to hang on to the tens of thousands of Italians working in agriculture and, if possible, to obtain even more Italians to supplement the decimated workforce at home.

Following capitulation, it was no longer politically acceptable for the Allies to ship Italians from Italy to other countries, although this still left large numbers of men held in camps in East and South Africa. However, transporting them to

Britain posed a huge logistical problem, while there was actually quite limited accommodation in which to house them.

Great debates were also taking place within the corridors of power about what sort of work the captured Italians could be given to do within the terms of the Geneva Convention, which gave no guidance concerning the service personnel of a country that had 'changed sides' during a conflict.

Like the Italians held in other camps throughout the UK, those in Orkney saw little or no change to their conditions during the months immediately following capitulation. They still had to be housed and fed somewhere and there was much work yet to be carried out on the causeways.

So, while the British, American and Italian Governments argued over the new status of Italian POWs, the men on Lamb Holm continued as they had since arriving on the island; working in the quarry to fill steel cages with stones, making concrete blocks at the block-making yard and dropping both items into the sea.

By the autumn of 1943, the barriers were solid constructions that men could walk across in all but rough weather. The inner core of bolsters had been protected by an outer layer of five-ton concrete blocks, dropped from the Blondins. Much of the design of the barriers was based on the results of research carried out using the cattle trough so many months earlier.

Separating the water had resulted in a complete change to the channels, where tides had once rushed through at frightening speeds. When the barriers

August 1943. Construction of the barrier across Kirk Sound, between Lamb Holm and mainland Orkney. Graemeshall is in the distance, on the right-hand side. *Source: Balfour Beatty.*

were only partially built and the same volume of sea tried to squeeze through an ever smaller opening, the noise and ferocity had been terrifying. It was as if something of great power had been made angry.

However, when the height of the barriers was raised sufficiently, so that the tide could no longer flow over the top, the water would rise and fall quite gently either side (normally at different levels). Underneath the surface, through thousands of small gaps and holes between the blocks and the bolsters, water continued to flow depending upon the tide.

The one aspect of the Italians' lives that did change for the better was that they had greater freedom to move around outside the camp. The general feeling amongst the men was that they were treated fairly and were well out of the war. There was no collective will to cause mischief or do harm. Their extra freedom was later to prove vital in their ability to obtain materials for the chapel. But all this was yet to take place and in the meantime the camp had its first priest, which was a beacon of great joy amongst the mainly Catholic POWs during a particularly difficult period.

7
The Chapel Begins

Following his capture, Padre Giacomo endured a similar fate to many of the other Italians in Camp 60 and was transferred between POW camps in North Africa before beginning a torturous route to England, in his case via Rhodesia, British Somaliland and Egypt. Eventually, on 9th September (the same day that the news of Italy's Capitulation was tearing through Camp 60), he ended up in Edinburgh with thirty other chaplains. The government's plan was to send the priests to the various Italian POW camps where they were needed most.

Padre Giacomo arrived on Lamb Holm on 30th September and he had to face the initial shock of the Orkney weather, just as his countrymen had done before him. In an *Orkney Herald* article he said:*

'What a difference from the African climate to the northern climate of Orkney — nights almost polar, intense cold, and what storms!'

But the weather aside, all the ingredients were now in one place to create a masterpiece, an icon of hope and peace that would later become famous around the world, when all the mess of war and construction had disappeared from the tiny island. There were many willing hands and skilled men amongst the POWs and they were lucky in having a camp commander who cared about their welfare.

* OA Ref 31/27/1

'The 500 Italians of Camp 60 were very happy at the arrival of the Chaplain of whom they were feeling the need. And I did my best to keep up their spirits and my own,' said Padre Giacomo.

It was really to raise the morale of the soldiers that I soon thought of providing the camp with a little church where they might meet in prayer, especially on Sundays for mass and the other sacred functions, knowing well how in adverse circumstances faith and religion have great power to help the human soul.

The soldiers were greatly pleased at my initiative, but naturally I had to obtain the approval of the Commandant of the Camp. At first the response was not favourable or, more exactly, the Commandant, Major Buckland, proposed to use a hut of corrugated iron meant for a school for the soldiers.

I did not lose heart. I had discovered that in the camp I had a very precious material — men who were true craftsmen. I then set them to work on the construction of the altar. In addition, I commissioned candlesticks, the cross and two lamps, all in wrought iron. The work went on almost in secret in their spare time and in poor light.

In Camp 60 there was a workshop in which work tools were repaired and the prisoners were set to do this. One morning, I remember the Commandant of the camp came to the workshop and saw the different pieces now accumulated for the candlesticks, the cross and lamps destined for the church. He looked at everything with curiosity and with great attention and also asked for explanations of the work.

I, who was present, was expecting not only a sharp rebuke followed by an order to stop everything, or even worse. The very reverse! Major Buckland was full of admiration for the work, which had been begun and he wished to show with deeds that he appreciated the art of the Italian craftsmen.

He took me to the school hut and said, 'Chaplain, arrange it as you wish for the chapel. For the location of the school we shall make other provision.'

Happy and enthusiastic, my artistic soldiers vied with each other to bring the work, begun almost clandestinely, to an end as soon as possible, and now carried on under the approval of the Commandant.

Years later, several people claimed the idea for building the chapel, and maybe they all had the thought in their heads and had held back from voicing it. The important point was that the determination and the skill existed and the project had the blessing of the authorities. In an interview for the Jam Jar Film documentary, Domenico made the following comment:

> When we landed in Orkney we found it very poor. It rained a lot and was very muddy. Little by little we settled and started to work things out. We worked and built paths between the sheds. It was not so bad then. We had the idea of the church because we had to satisfy our inner need for religion. Our conscience as Christians urged us to have something spiritual to face the horrors of the world, to pray for the end of the war.

It was around the time when discussions were still taking place about how best to proceed that Major Buckland called Domenico into his office and initiated a conversation that resulted in a situation of total misunderstanding, which we may laugh at looking back. Domenico, who spoke very little English, later explained what happened in an article in the *Orkney Herald*, published a few weeks after the one by Padre Giacomo in 1959.*

> Major Buckland called me to his office and, in his halting Italian, explained to me that we could make some sort of chapel. I told him that if I did it at all I should do it really well. The major didn't understand — in fact, he thought that I was refusing and, annoyed, he called the interpreter. When the misunderstanding had been cleared up, he slapped me on the back and said 'Bravo! Make a good job of it.' That was how the work started.

The most pressing problem was whether to build the chapel from scratch

* *OA Ref 31/27/1*

or convert something already existing. The first option would require much greater time, effort and materials, but all the huts in Camp 60 were in use and there was nothing that could be spared. Major Buckland's authority was limited outside the camp but in a letter* to Ernest Marwick, written in March 1959, he explained how the huts were obtained:

> Colonel Lynch, P/W (prisoner of war) Inspector of Camps from the War Office, had been urging us to build a chapel and then came Padre Giacobazzi. He arrived with great hope of finding a suitable building. Eventually, Mr G. G. Nicol — you will no doubt remember him — gave us two huts. We joined the two using one end for the church and the other for a school. As soon as this was done the P/W started using the hut for religious and educational purposes.

Gordon Nicol was the resident superintending civil engineer overseeing the construction of the barriers from March 1942 onwards. He had taken a keen interest in the well-being of the men working on this great project and his remit gave him much greater access to resources, a fact that was to prove vital in the creation of the chapel.

Back in Italy, the newly formed Badoglio Government openly declared war on Germany on 13th October. This turned everything on its head. Italy's former allies were now officially the enemy. Exactly what status should be given to Italy continued to present enormous problems to the British Government and its allies.

Some thought that a country that had so recently been an enemy could not be considered an ally. Eventually the country was given the title of 'co-belligerent', although what this actually meant was not clear. There was certainly plenty of confusion in the Orkney camps, as men waited to hear whether they were even POWs anymore.

The idea of building a chapel took on more importance and Camp 60 was alive with excitement as men discussed the possibilities at every opportunity.

* OA Ref 31/27/2

Domenico gathered his team of craftsmen. Today, these men are either known to have passed away or their whereabouts are unknown. There are slight variations in who is believed to have carried out which specific task, depending upon whose version of the events you read.

What is certain is that the stonemason was Domenico Buttapasta and the blacksmith, Giuseppe Palumbi. Assunto Micheloni and Michele De Vitto were electricians and a man called Sforza was a carpenter. Barcaglioni and Battiato were bricklayers. There were many others who helped — Sergeant Primavera, Esposito, even Sergeant Major Fornasier were involved.

During November, a group of men dug the foundations at the site chosen for the chapel, near the camp gates. The plan was to have the chapel entrance facing west, into the camp's centre, which would put the chancel, altar and vestry at the east, in the direction of Holm Sound and the North Sea.

Even at this early stage, enthusiasm for the chapel was so infectious that it spread beyond the boundaries of the barbed-wire perimeter fence, beyond the borders of religion, beliefs and nationalities. When they were approached, Balfour Beatty readily offered to donate the required concrete, so at the end of one working day a dumper truck duly arrived and the foundations were laid.

The two Nissen huts sourced by Gordon Nicol were emptied of their contents, and later in November they were carried to their new home by gangs of Italians working in relays and joined together to create one building, 16 x 72 feet in size. This was quickly secured into the concrete base to stop it from being blown away in the fierce winds that blew across the islands — the fate of more than one hut during stormy weather.

The Italians had their building. It had a door at each end, with two windows within the brickwork either side of the doors. There were two dormer windows down each side of the building. Apart from cement they had virtually no materials to hand and little money to purchase anything with.

It is difficult to imagine today just what they thought at that time, as they stood inside their new building, which was essentially another tin shack. What vision did they see in their mind's eye? Certainly, it wasn't what was eventually created, because that was the result of a series of different projects, as one part of the chapel was completed and it was decided to convert another area.

The original purpose of creating a larger building was to use one end as a chapel and the other for classes. Camp 60 held many highly educated Italians and the men were eager to organise regular classes. Some attempts had been made, using the mess hall, but to have something dedicated to this purpose was considered a better solution all round.

As their second Christmas in Orkney approached, the chapel took on a new dimension for the Italians. It became more than just a focus, more than something to do that was better than a hobby. It became many things; perhaps best summed up by ex-POW Bruno Volpi. In a letter sent to Alastair and Anne Cormack, which they reproduced in *Bolsters Blocks Barriers*, Bruno said:

I cannot but agree with the beauty and professional skill that many sources, from newspaper to tourist brochures, attribute to the works of art on Lamb Holm and with the feeling of almost palpable love that those artists seem to have instilled into their creations. There is something, though, that I'd like to point out.

What is it that made prisoners of war work so feverishly with partially or totally inadequate means at their disposal? It was the wish to show to oneself first, and to the world then, that in spite of being trapped in a barbed wired camp, down in spirit physically and morally deprived of many things, one could still find something inside that could be set free.

People cannot be judged by their precarious situations. Their culture, spirit and will to express themselves in creative thoughts and deeds are stronger than any limitation to freedom. This is the spirit that gave birth to the works of art on Lamb Holm.

The statue of St George was built first. It shows the patron saint of soldiers ready to kill the dragon. It is a concrete representation of the desire to eliminate all evil, all wars that cause pain and injustice to so many people. It is the symbol of a will to 'kill' all misunderstandings among people of different cultures.

As the St George was built to express the physical and psychological pain, so was the chapel conceived to meet a spiritual need.

But all this was to come. What they had by the Christmas of 1943 was an empty Nissen hut . . . and endless supplies of cement.

8
The Chancel

The beginning of 1944 was a worrying time for the men in the Orkney camps because Italy was more of a battlefield than ever. The Allies had been pushing the German army further north inch by inch since the previous July, but at a huge cost to both sides and everything around them. Now the Germans were dug in across a line that ran from the Sangro River in the east to a little north of the Garigliano River to the west.

It was the famous Gustav Line, which cut across the main road north to Rome at a point near to the town of Cassino and the historic monastery of Monte Cassino. During February, the old abbey was destroyed in heavy bombing by the Allies, who feared that the enemy was using the views from the building, high on a hill, to its advantage. Soon afterwards, a major Allied force landed at Anzio, which opened up a new front of fierce fighting on Italian soil. Gino recounts the general feeling amongst the men in Camp 34:

> We carried on as usual but with bitterness inside our souls. We were very worried about our dear ones' destiny. Latina [Gino's home] is very close to Anzio and after the Allied landing in the area there had been hard fighting and heavy bombing. We had no news of family. I leave it to your imagination how we felt.

Yet again the winter was cruel, and the work on the causeways was relentless. The pace of work on the chapel increased. The risk of damp seeping through the sections of the corrugated-iron sheeting was a real danger, so the first task was to build a wooden frame against the inside walls. Every job presented a hurdle that had to be jumped, even obtaining materials for this relatively simple piece of woodwork. However, eventually the framework was completed and included a stud wall, which would later enable a vestry to be built, as well as a wall against which to place the altar. The vestry walls were never intended to be lined, and even today they are simply the inside corrugated iron walls of a standard Second World War Nissen hut, painted in magnolia.

The dividing wall incorporated gaps for two small lancet windows, positioned either side of the altar. Glass was obtained and one of the carpenters made the windows. An opening was left for a door to the left of the altar that would enable the priest to enter the chancel from the vestry. One of the carpenters fitted a door. No efforts were to be spared in making the chancel as impressive as possible, although finding plasterboard at that point proved too difficult. Instead, pressed cardboard was fixed to the wooden frame.

Major Buckland's help and enthusiasm for the project was crucial and he provided a link to the outside world when it came to sourcing materials. The rule that stated the Italians could not receive 'real' money was relaxed and they started a 'chapel fund' using money generated from the sale of the items they made. Money also came from the sale of goods in the camp canteen, which was run along NAAFI (Navy, Army & Air Force Institutes) lines, although staffed by Italians. A percentage of everything sold went into the chapel fund.

The Italians were paid in camp tokens for the work they did and they could spend these at the canteen. Unskilled men received tokens equivalent to one shilling per day and skilled men one shilling and six pence. Tokens were handed out once a week in the mess hall. At the time, a Balfour Beatty civilian worker on the project would be paid about six pounds a week.

There is a story that a local artist heard about the Italians' venture and donated brushes and jars of poster paints, although it has been impossible to confirm this. Certainly, later on, Domenico obtained some supplies from J. M. Stevenson in Kirkwall, and became friendly with the manager, Ernest Marwick. He was able to create a myriad of colours from the poster paints, which could be mixed on a palette.

With these, Domenico created what many consider to be the focal point of the entire chapel, his painting of the Madonna and Child above the altar. Throughout the war, Domenico had carried a small religious card that had been given to him by his mother before he left Moena. The card depicted an image based on a well-known painting by Italian artist Nicolò Barabino (1832–1891) of the Madonna and Child.

Domenico used the little religious card as a guide for his painting, although he added significantly to the original image. The central part of the reredos shows a likeness of the Blessed Virgin holding the infant Jesus in her arms, who is offering his mother an olive branch, the symbol of peace. Both are enveloped by the white folds of her clothing and surrounded by a golden background, a symbolic reflection from their haloes.

Domenico surrounded the image of the Blessed Virgin with six cherubim, holding a scroll that is inscribed *'Regina pacis ora pro nobis'* (Queen of Peace pray for us). Sadly, the actual card that Domenico carried with him throughout the war, and took with him back to Italy, was lost years later. However, John Muir had a copy and the wording on the reverse translates as:

Oh Jesus, you said: 'I have come to bring the fire (of charity) to the earth, and what else do I want if not that it be kindled?' Oh let men, overcoming individual and national egoisms, recognise themselves as brothers, may they refrain from discord, may they love and help one another and form one heart with Your heart in loving, praising and blessing the common Father who is in heaven, to whom is all honour and glory now and for ever. Amen.

'I carried a little picture of the Madonna of the Olive Branch with me everywhere and this was the inspiration for the central picture,' said Domenico.

The rest of the picture, the head of the angel, the four evangelists and, at the sides, angels kneeling in adoration, I created myself. The war was still going on and naturally the motif which inspired me was peace. On the left, an angel held the heraldic badge of Moena in his hand, a man rowing his boat out of the storm towards the calm sea. On the right, another angel was sheathing his sword.

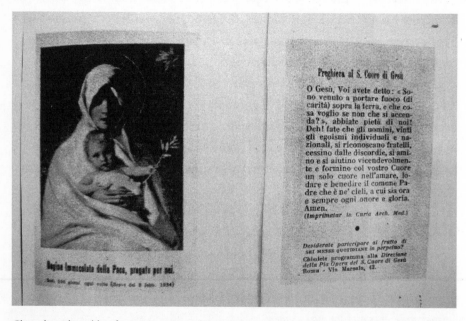

Chiocchetti based his famous painting of the Madonna and Child on a small prayer card. It was given to him by his mother and he carried it with him throughout the war. The card was lost years later but this is a replica of the one he had.

Nicolò Barabino's painting is often referred to as the *Madonna of the Olives* but many versions along similar themes were created, including one entitled *Madonna of the Lemons*. It proved to be extremely difficult to ascertain the correct title for the picture that Domenico reproduced. In the end, emailing a photograph of the painting above the altar to the National Gallery of Scotland resulted in a reply from Aidan Weston-Lewis, Chief Curator, Italian and Spanish Art.

> In truth, images of this kind are generally referred to simply as the *Madonna and Child* or *Virgin and Child*. In this case, however, we have a little more to go on. The image is obviously from a devotional or prayer book and the illustration is accompanied by the text *Vergine Immacolata della Pace* — The Immaculate Virgin of Peace. The Christ Child holds an olive sprig, a common symbol of peace in Christian imagery.

Domenico was keen to make the altar and he managed to acquire a quantity of clay from mainland Orkney, a material not available on Lamb Holm. From this, he moulded the shape of the altar and subsequently made a cast in plaster of Paris into which he poured concrete. The stout legs of the altar resemble Doric columns and contrast well with the more delicate open fretwork that stretches between the two front legs. The design of the fretwork is similar to the imaginative 'stonework' in the chancel and brings together these different elements so that they appear to have one designer, one creator, which they did.

On the wall between the two rear legs he painted a red background and, in the centre, in large gold letters, 'IHS', to represent the Body of Christ. The altar, painted white, stands on a rectangular area that is raised above the chancel floor, which is itself higher than the rest of the floor in the building.

These areas were made from the seemingly never-ending supply of concrete. For the base directly under the altar, the men added stone chips to give the surface a textured feel, and the appearance almost of marble. Domenico then started work on the altar rail, while other men worked to create different objects for the chancel.

'The good Major Buckland did everything he could to get us paints and brushes,' said Domenico.

I painted St Francis of Assisi and St Catherine of Siena on the glass of the windows and outlined the panes so that they seemed to be made of lead. As soon as the altar was ready, Padre Giacobazzi celebrated mass, accompanied by a small harmonium which the major had somehow or other obtained for us. We sang the Gregorian mass and I was part of the choir.

The painting on the window to the right of the altar is the image of St Francis of Assisi, while that on the left-hand side is St Catherine of Siena. The latter was born in 1347 and became an advocate for peace. During her lifetime, she was known at the highest levels in both the church and governments of Europe. St Francis was born in 1181 and, following an earlier career as a soldier, he renounced his wealth and inheritance to dedicate his life to the sick and preach the words of Jesus Christ. In 1209, he founded the Franciscans.

Domenico painted these figures on the vestry side of the glass, both facing inwards to look up at the Madonna and Child. On the chancel side he painted strips, which give the impression of depth and makes the illusion of leaded glass more realistic. The overall effect is to make the figures look as if they are set within a gothic niche in the wall, whereas the wall behind the altar is completely flat. It's an excellent example of Domenico's skill at *trompe-l'oeil*: a way to trick the eye into seeing a three-dimensional object from a two-dimensional painting.

So the men in Camp 60 had an altar, complete with reredos and candlesticks. Padre Giacomo held his first mass. It was certainly better than using the mess hall but this was only the start of what was later created. Domenico continued to paint the rest of the chancel.

At the start of the First World War, the British had sunk a significant number of old ships in the narrower channels leading into Scapa Flow in an attempt to block these entrances to the enemy. Some were removed after the war to provide access to the North Sea as fishing villages such as St Mary's had been hit hard by the closure. Many more blockships were added in the lead up to the Second

While the chancel was being built, work continued on the causeways. Here, a crane is placing five-ton blocks in Weddell Sound. *Source: Balfour Beatty.*

World War, when Scapa Flow was once again chosen as the main harbour for the British Home Fleet.

Even in times of war, these old ships were beyond any useful life. However, they still contained a significant amount of materials that were simply left behind — glass, tiles, wood, metals — which provided a valuable source to the Italians on their doorstep, or rather under it!

'Sergeant Primavera made two candelabra from brass obtained from the stairs of a wrecked ship,' said Domenico.

The bottom of the sea provided us with much of the iron that we used and with the wood for the tabernacle and the stones for the floor. There were no divers amongst us that I remember.

There was a half-sunk ship. When the tide was low we used to get into the ship. We found glass, iron, tiles and wood . . . wood for the tabernacle of the altar. It took us one year to find all the materials. The commander allowed us to bring all of this stuff up.

At a certain place, which would later be the start of the Lamb Holm end of barrier number two, the British had rammed the old ship *Lycia* on to rocks as part of an attempt to block Skerry Sound. In a line behind the *Lycia* was the old German ship, *Ilsenstein* and behind this lay *Emerald Wings*. All three blockships had been positioned there during 1940. It was possible to climb a ladder to the deck of the *Lycia* and walk across to the *Ilsenstein* but the *Emerald Wings* was too far out and submerged to reach.

Getting into and out of these partly sunken ships was not without its dangers. With the tide racing at more than ten knots, the sea would often pour across the decks. In a quote reproduced in *Bolsters Blocks Barriers*, Gordon Nicol gives a vivid description of the conditions around the blockships before the creation of the barriers.

At the time of high water spring tides the roar of the currents, boiling around, under and sometimes over the blockships was like that of a mighty waterfall and on a sunny day the colours merged from deepest purple to palest green with pure white spray leaping in the air.

The tide could drop so rapidly that fish were often left stranded on the decks and it was common for the Italians to simply gather these in buckets and take them back to camp to supplement their diet. The attraction of something valuable under the decks was too great for many and men would often explore the accessible parts. There is no record of anyone coming to harm because of this practice.

The chancel floor consists of red, black and white squares and it is documented that this was created by the stonemason Buttapasta, using tiles he had discovered in a bathroom in the *Ilsenstein*, a 1,500-ton German steamer built in 1898. Buttapasta removed the tiles carefully, one by one, cleaned them and laid them in a pattern, just as they can be seen to this day.

The question arose at some point during the research for this book, 'Did Buttapasta bring three sets of tiles off the ship?' Kneeling on the chancel floor, tapping gently and feeling the temperature and surface texture of the floor, resulted in the conclusion that Buttapasta's tiles make up the black and white squares, while the red squares are actually painted concrete.

The Italians in Camp 34 had more opportunity to meet local people than their fellow countrymen on Lamb Holm and Gino Caprara made many Orcadian friends who have kept in touch over the years. The natural friendliness of Orcadians greatly touched the Italians, as Gino explained:

I was introduced to the Wylie family and they invited me to their home, where we had a cup of tea and a long friendly chat. They showed me kindness and were astonished at my English. I myself was deeply moved for being treated so kindly after some three years of internment. When we left, they said to me, 'Come again, come again.'

Now, being of a moderate and discreet character I did not avail myself of the invitation, fearing to be too invasive. But one evening, when we were all allowed to go out, I had a surprise. Mr Wylie was near the gate waiting for me and addressed me as follows: 'What is wrong with you? Why did you not pay a visit to us? Have you been ill?'

I told him that I was afraid of being too invasive. He said: 'Don't be silly! Come with me.' I received a very warm welcome from Mrs Ina and we enjoyed a lovely supper. It is difficult for me to describe my feelings. For years, we had been looked at with suspicion, distrust and sometimes with hate . . . to be received in that way, it gave me back confidence in mankind.

As the Italians proved their worth, and civilian workers continued to be conscripted or sent south to work on even more urgent building projects, an increasing number of skilled Italians took over jobs from the construction workers, becoming crane operators, lorry drivers and even train drivers. As such, they became more integrated with the Balfour Beatty men.

Machines and men were pushed to the limit in the quest to build the causeways and one of the cranes toppled over having been used to try and lift a load that was too heavy. Apparently, the Italian crane driver was more concerned about the trinkets he had been making earlier than about himself!

Sixty Italians were moved to a camp of the Royal Pioneer Corps near Stromness, where their labour was needed in the local dockyards. They would remain working there, separated from the other Italians in Orkney until the end of the war, when they would be moved to camps in England.

Several men had acquired bikes that were often considered to be beyond repair by the previous owners. However, in the hands of determined men who had been engineers and skilled tradesmen before the war, these bikes were given a new lease on life in the Camp 60 workshop.

With farms in Orkney short of labour, small gangs of Italians were sometimes taken under escort to help clear ditches, put up fences or other general work. Many of the men had been farmers and felt an immediate affinity with both the work and the Orkney countryside. There is a story of an Italian taking the reins of a horse and plough out of the farmer's hands and ploughing a perfectly straight furrow, much to the surprise of those standing around.

Quite early on, the research uncovered a lady in Bromley who had enjoyed a keen interest in the chapel since a child, and many friendships with the people involved with it. Her name is Lesley McLetchie.

'I spent my childhood in Orkney and remember my grandmother taking me to the chapel when I was eight, which would have been 1945,' said Lesley.

> I danced around the statue of St George, not realising the danger of the nearby barbed wire, and ended up being quite badly cut. However, we still went into the chapel and that's when my love for the building began. At that time, the door into the vestry wasn't locked and so I poked my head inside. It was full of pots of paint and tools.

Lesley left Orkney to attend boarding school but kept in touch with friends from the islands and even today she gets the *Orcadian* newspaper and *Living Orkney* magazine sent to her home.

> In the mid-eighties I read an article in the *Orcadian* from a man called Rocco Bernacchio. He was talking about the chapel and the Italian POWs. I wrote to him and from that one piece of correspondence I became involved with the ex-POW Association for Camp 60 and Camp 34, attending their last meeting in Italy as a guest.

Lesley told of chapels built by Italian POWs in Henllan, West Wales and Letterkenny, in America. She wasn't sure if the latter still existed but it sparked a new trail of research. Letterkenny is in Pennsylvania. The nearest place found with an email address was West College so they were contacted, to ask if they could help. The reply was that the chapel had nothing to do with the college but, yes, it was still there. The sender suggested a contact and, several emails later, the current owners of the chapel were found: the United Churches of Chambersburg, who confirmed that the building is still in use.

Lesley had built up quite a collection of material relevant to the Orkney chapel over the years, including correspondence, newspaper cuttings, contact addresses and copies of minutes of the ex-POW Association. She is also an avid poet and the building on Lamb Holm has inspired her on more than one occasion. One of her poems is printed on the next page.

Madonna of the Olives
(Italian Chapel, Lamb Holm, Orkney)

Italian sunshine gleams in a northern island.
A spirit of Renaissance in a house of God
fashioned from Nissen huts and scraps.
Bleakness and grey mists are not synonymous
with gaiety and warmth,
but fused they are in this island chapel.

Here prisoners of war planned not how to escape
but how to build a place of worship.
Do not look for the bully beef tin in the
perfectly carved light shade.
Do not look for cast-off materials
in the frescoes and fittings.
Rather see the richness of inspiration revealed
in the altar and rood screen,
wrought with such loving hands.

Strange that the Italian warmth should strike one
in this windswept barren island.
Yet here in this chapel is knowledge of faith,
hope and love in adversity. Would that the
serenity of Barabino's Madonna encompass us
as we face the bleakness of the world outside.

Regina pacis. Ora pro nobis

Lesley M. McLetchie

9
The Rood Screen

In 1928, Giuseppe Palumbi travelled from Teramo in Italy to Philadelphia to join his father Nicola, who had moved to America looking for work eight years earlier. The seventeen-year-old Giuseppe learnt English and the art of *ferro battuto* — wrought-iron work. At the time, the area was a major centre for producing iron and Giuseppe learnt techniques for heating and working the material that were similar to those used in Italy during the Renaissance.

He stayed in America until 1932, but hated the gruelling work, for which he was poorly paid and consequently always hungry. After his return he often voiced his opinion that the ideals of communism would be the answer to Italy's problems, a dangerous point of view to talk of openly during the 1930s.

One day he met a friend for coffee and the man dragged him into the back of the café, where he said that Giuseppe's openly expressed views had put his life in great danger. His only way out was to enlist. Giuseppe took the threat so seriously that he went home, said goodbye to his wife Pierina and two-year-old son Renato, and later that day joined Mussolini's army. Like the others in Camp 60, he was captured during the North African campaigns. In his case, he had been in Bardia when taken prisoner.

The skills he gained during his time in Philadelphia were to enable him to create one of the wonders of the chapel, the beautiful rood screen that can still be admired today. However, when he first arrived on Lamb Holm it was Giuseppe's ability to speak English that set him apart from most of the other Italians, and he was often called upon to translate or help out in difficult situations.

He joined Domenico's team of craftsmen and, early in 1944, the idea of building the rood screen came into being. It was needed to separate the planned highly ornate chancel from the rest of the unattractive Nissen hut, which was not intended to be converted originally. But first of all, Giuseppe would have to build a forge.

There is very little information on how he achieved this, but it is probably fair to assume that he made use of the ready supply of local stone and cement. He must have been given a hut to build it in, most likely donated by Balfour Beatty or sourced by Gordon Nicol.

In order to gain a greater understanding of how Giuseppe would have gone about this whole task of creating the rood screen, the blacksmith on South Ronaldsay was approached.

Eighty-three-year-old Willie Mowat, MBE, is a man with an immense

Giuseppe Palumbi with his wife, Pierina, and son, Renato. Taken in Morro d'Oro, 1947.

knowledge of the art of blacksmithing and he is, as he said himself, one of the last of a dying breed. At the age of eleven, he had stood opposite his father with a mallet in his hands and learnt the art of beating the glowing metal, synchronising his strokes with those of his father's, while the rod was turned by someone else.

'If you were a split second out it could result in a nasty accident . . . so you learnt the importance of timing,' said Willie.

His smithy is a piece of living history; built by his great grandfather, it is a treasure trove of bygone days. None of Willie's own sons have followed him into the craft and it is hoped that when he dies the building will be taken over by an organisation to preserve it for the future.

Picking up a mallet, the large head made silver from years of use, he made the room come alive with ringing by hitting one of the larger anvils from its horn to the heel and back again. Never having heard an anvil sing, this unexpected demonstration led to the idea for the scene in *The Italian Chapel* when Giuseppe makes the anvil sing.

Sam Moore Barlow, a Highland artist specialising in metals, provided advice on the sort of materials that would have been available during the war:

The types of iron rods that were used as reinforcement bars at the time would have been the sweepings of the junkyard — a mixture of old farm machinery, railings, pots and pans — all melted together.

The resulting low quality steel bars would react differently along their length as they were heated and worked at the forge, with the impurities creating brittle sections and the risk of the steel burning or breaking.

It would be very difficult for the blacksmith to gauge how the metal was going to react at any point and, of course, each bar would be different to the one before. He would have been faced with quite a challenge to say the least.

Giuseppe Palumbi was reunited with his wife Pierina and young son Renato when he was repatriated in 1945. He died in 1980 but a letter to Renato resulted in a reply shortly afterwards from the blacksmith's grandson, also called

Giuseppe, but known as 'Pino'. Renato did not speak English, but was keen that the story should be told about his father's time in Orkney and the rood screen he made for the famous chapel.

It was a subject father and son had spoken about often and Renato was willing to write down as much as he could remember. Pino and his wife, Ivana, would translate the notes into English. This was the beginning of a correspondence with Pino that continues today.

There are various accounts as to where the iron came from that was used in the rood screen, with some articles saying they were reinforcement rods used within the concrete blocks and others that they were taken from the boiler of a blockship. Renato said that his father had told him the rods were donated by Balfour Beatty and were from stock used in the construction of local buildings.

In Lamb Holm they gave him the iron used to build houses, most of it was round and unfortunately for him had many stainless steel parts. The work was very hard because he had to work the iron to its very limits but without breaking it. This job was done in the same way as in the Middle Ages.

It is a testament to Giuseppe's skill and determination that he created a masterpiece that equals anything else in the chapel. Following a design drawn by Domenico, Giuseppe created an intricate display of swirls, leaves and patterns that is both functional and stunning.

The screen stretches across the entire width of the building, following the curve of the walls and ceiling, making it ten feet high in the middle and sixteen feet across. The lower section, which is about three feet high, contains two wrought-iron gates, one containing the initials 'IHS' and the other the word 'Maria', a common inscription in a Catholic church.

The upper portion incorporates three arches. The central, largest arch provides a frame for the altar and the painting of the Madonna and Child to anyone standing in the nave. It took Giuseppe four months to build the rood screen, working full-time at the forge.

Major Buckland had agreed that the key craftsmen working on the chapel could spend all their time on this task, as long as their work on the barriers was covered by other men. Such was the dedication of the Italians that this was not an issue, with men (including non-Catholics and non-believers) readily offering to cover for those directly involved in the creation of the chapel.

In later years, Giuseppe often referred to the enormous task he was given in building the rood screen, saying how it was the greatest and most complex creation he ever made. He brought back to Italy a photograph of the screen after the war and hung it on a wall in his house. Renato said:

Sometimes I surprised him, when he was staring at the picture. I understood he had left part of his heart on the island. He was very worried that anybody would ever ask him to take on again a job like the one in the chapel. One day in front of St Peter's in Rome, he was staring at the big gate in *ferro battuto*, and said, 'I could have done that!'

In a letter to John Muir, Renato makes several very poignant comments about how his father wanted to return to Orkney.

Every single moment his mind went back there, on that 'rock', which he thought abandoned, where he had left the proof of how much he was worth. Every time it was as though he wanted to say, 'Let's go back and see it.' That picture has always been there, on the wall, and lots of times I have been surprised by my father's melancholy look. Is it possible that a prison becomes so important? I can answer that it's possible when only there have you been able to express your potential in a complete way.

However, the greatest surprise in more than four years of research was an email from Pino revealing that his grandfather, while living in Orkney, had fallen in love with a local woman. (The woman Giuseppe loved was never tracked down and was called 'Fiona' in *The Italian Chapel*. This is not her real name.)

In Renato's notes, received after Pino's startling revelation, he makes reference to how they met:

This image of the rood screen has been captured thousands of times. This particular photograph, showing a harmonium in the right-hand corner, was the one that Palumbi took back to Italy after the war and hung on a wall in his home. He could be found staring at the image in silence many times during the remainder of his life. *Photograph by James W. Sinclair.*

The English brought the iron and carbon needed for the forge to Lamb Holm in a boat. Often they allowed him [Giuseppe] to take a boat and go to the mainland. In one of these trips he met Fiona. She was twenty years old. She played the piano very well and he played the banjo, which he bought with the money he made by selling lighters that he built out of aluminium.

Many times he was invited for lunch by Fiona's family and one day they said to him that some English newspapers described these young Italian fascists as Nazi criminals. They were surprised because now they had met him they understood that the newspapers lied.

When he returned home in 1945 Giuseppe told his wife about Fiona and even showed a photograph of her, which Pierina promptly burned. However, they stayed together and, in 1950, had a second child. When this daughter had a baby girl some twenty years later, she named her after the woman in Orkney that her father had loved.

It was, said Pino — who had never realised the significance of his cousin's name until translating his father's notes — 'the realisation of a little part of his dream.' He was very close to his granddaughter.

The greatest secret in the chapel is in plain view to anyone stepping into the chancel but it is, at the same time, so cleverly disguised that few people would ever see it.

Orkney tour guide Dr Francis Roberts is passionate about the building. He is also a native speaker of Italian, as his mother is Italian and Francis grew up in Eritrea where, by coincidence, Padre Giacomo landed in 1935. During research for *The Italian Chapel*, Francis had made a passing reference to the 'heart of the chapel', but gave no details.

The next day, it took a thorough search to find it. But there it was. With the knowledge of Giuseppe's feelings for Fiona, it was immediately clear that the heart was a token the blacksmith had left behind for the woman he loved: a heart-shaped piece of wrought iron embedded into the floor, the stop for the two gates in the rood screen.

When the gates were shut it was impossible to tell the shape. It was only when they were opened that the heart was revealed. Of course, anyone walking into the chancel would be looking at the images on the walls and the painting above the altar, not at their feet.

Photographs were taken and emailed to Pino as soon as possible. He sent another excited email in return.

'It's exactly my grandfather's behaviour. He was a very private man, the same as the iron heart, but when you open the gate you find a hidden, little-big, romantic heart. This is the meaning of the iron heart.'

Giuseppe continued to work as a blacksmith upon his repatriation to Italy, but in the post-war period people did not want to pay much for this sort of work and times were difficult for a while. He died at the age of sixty-nine in 1980, never achieving his wish of returning to Orkney, but the rood screen remains one of the wonders of the chapel. His wife Pierina died in 2000.

The spelling of Giuseppe's surname has caused much confusion over the years. In Padre Giacomo's article, published in 1959 in the *Orkney Herald*, he refers to the blacksmith who built the rood screen as 'Palumbi'. A few weeks later in the article from Domenico, this is spelt 'Palumbo'.

Ever since, virtually all articles, whether in newspapers, magazines or on websites, have used the latter spelling. It was only in 2001, when Renato contacted John Muir to organise a family trip to the chapel, that the correct spelling could finally be confirmed.

10
The Chasm

Like other Italian POWs, the men in Camp 60 had been given virtually no information on what Italy's Capitulation the previous September meant to them and there was a feeling of great frustration at the lack of news or of change to their lives. However, any decisions along these lines were in the hands of the British Government, which remained locked in discussions with the American and Italian Governments over the status of the Italians in their charge.

It was an uncertain period for everyone. Back in Italy, Italian servicemen who had been captured by the Allies during their invasion of Sicily the previous July had subsequently been released to help out with the harvest. But by the end of the year, many Italian units operating further north, which had never been captured, ended up fighting their previous partners, the Germans.

One day in April, the men lined up on the Camp 60 parade ground to hear Major Buckland announce they had the chance to become 'volunteer cooperatives' and be formed into Italian Labour Battalions. Those accepting this offer would receive better conditions. They would be paid in British coinage, rather than camp tokens and it could even be arranged for this money to be sent home to their families via the Protecting Power.

Some would receive an increase in pay, with skilled men being paid nine shillings a week and unskilled men seven shillings. Italian NCOs would receive even more. Deductions would not be made if a man was sick, while mealtimes and travel to the place of work would be considered as 'work time'.

If the men agreed, the Lamb Holm camp would be reclassified as a Labour Battalion, although it would retain its Camp 60 number. Volunteer cooperatives would be issued with chestnut-coloured uniforms with the word 'Italy' on the shoulder. These men would continue to live in the camp, but would no longer be escorted by armed guards to that day's place of work. Instead they would be taken by their own NCOs. The perimeter fence would be dismantled and during daylight hours men would be able to exercise outside.

Italians who did not wish to accept the offer would continue to be treated as POWs and would be moved to another, more suitable camp as soon as possible. The changes would come into effect on 1st May.

Although the majority were pragmatic about the deal and felt that they might as well be paid for the work they did (and have better living conditions) there was a hard core in both camps who were determined to remain loyal to Mussolini. Fierce arguments broke out almost immediately between the two groups, even between men who had been friends long before ever arriving in Orkney. After more than sixty years, the hurt felt by Gino Caprara is still raw.

Those who decided not to accept the conditions would be considered POWs and receive the same treatment they had had until now, but would be transferred to an appropriate camp. He [the camp commander] gave us one hour to decide. Considering that we had always worked and should have continued to work with better conditions, almost all of us decided to form an Italian Labour Battalion. In our camp only fifteen men did not accept the proposal and after two days they left Orkney to be transferred elsewhere.

It is very sad to remember that friends with whom we had lived in harmony for years, at the moment of their departure, instead of giving us a brotherly farewell, greeted us with the following insult: 'Sold out to the enemy.' Some of us insulted them in reply: 'Dirty fascists!' What a shame. It was a very painful experience.

In his letter written in 1959 to Ernest Marwick, the retired Lt Colonel Buckland said:

When the Italians withdrew from the war the prisoners were asked to become cooperators and although they had protested on being sent so far north on their arrival on the island of Lamb Holm, ninety-seven per cent agreed to cooperate.

This meant around fifteen men in each camp remained loyal to Mussolini and were moved from Orkney. In some Italian POW camps in Britain the two groups were almost evenly split. This posed a huge logistical problem for the British Government, which had to move men so that each camp contained only those of either co-volunteers or POWs. The potential for conflict was too great to leave both sides living and working together.

So for the meantime, the Italians in Orkney carried on as they had for the last two years. Conditions in the camp had certainly improved and this continued,

Barrier number two in June 1944 between Lamb Holm and Glimps Holm. *Source: Balfour Beatty.*

although some of the improvements promised by the government were slow to materialise.

There was greater interaction between the men in the camps and local service personnel. Football matches became a regular event and these included games between the Italians and the British soldiers who manned nearby anti-aircraft batteries. However, these did not always help relationships between the two sides, as Gino explained:

I would like to describe what happened during one of these matches. One of our forwards was heavily hindered by a British defender who completely ignored fair play. At a certain moment, our player, tired of being impeded so heavily, shouted to his antagonist, '*Ora Basta!*' In Italian it means, 'Stop it. Enough!' The British soldier, misunderstanding the meaning of the word, angrily asked, 'Bastard? To me?' The answer was, 'Yes!'

I let you imagine what happened ... punches, kicks, violent pushes. Other Italian and British players took part in the fray. In short, there was an invasion of the pitch by the Italian and British spectators. The sentries tried to put down the struggle by blowing their whistles. At last, the mess came to an end and once the misunderstanding was explained, the two men shook hands. The result of that event was that we were punished by being confined to barracks for one week!

Of course, there are two sides to every story and local man John Rosie recalled the football matches in his interview with Jam Jar Films.

Later on, when the barriers were open, the Italians had more freedom and they would come over to St Mary's to play football with the local boys. They were very good footballers. Perhaps you don't always remember their names but you remember the ones who kicked you the hardest! It was the first time I had ever seen the overhead kick. They were very good players, but a bit quick in their temper.

11
The Chancel is Complete

Padre Giacomo started holding mass in the 'chapel' as soon as the altar was completed and he was often accompanied by the carpenter Sforza on a harmonium, presumably borrowed from a local family. But his were not the only services to be held in the building. The Reverend John Davies, who had arrived in May as the local army chaplain, held a service once a fortnight in the Lamb Holm chapel for local British soldiers, any non-Catholics amongst the Italians and anyone else who wanted to attend.

For a time, the Reverend Davies had thirty-six camps within his area and, as active service personnel, had to be less than two minutes away from 'action stations'. He conducted services in venues that were varied in every sense, from a mess hall to a bar.

The craftsmen continued to transform the chancel end of the Nissen hut. Salvaged wood from one of the blockships was used to line the bottom half of each side of the chancel, between the vestry wall and the altar rail. Panels of wood, shaped like arches, were stained to create blind arcading against the lighter wood behind.

Domenico made an altar rail in the same way that he made the altar, moulding the shape he wanted in clay before making a plaster-of-Paris cast and filling this with concrete. The altar rail, painted white to match the altar, rests along the edge of the raised chancel floor and even the open structure conveys strength and permanence.

Between the altar rail and the edge of the chancel, where Palumbi's rood screen would eventually stand, the carpenters added a dado with compressed board fixed to a horizontal wooden frame below. Domenico painted the board in shades of grey to resemble stone panels, some of which showed sheaves of wheat and others bunches of grapes. These represented the bread and wine as used in the Eucharist, which was celebrated regularly by Padre Giacomo.

Giuseppe made two wrought-iron candlesticks, which were added to the four that Sergeant Primavera had made out of brass (he added two more to the original two he made). The Italian sergeant also made lanterns out of used bully-beef tins.

It was the painting of the chancel that made the greatest difference and this work fell on to the shoulders of the artist from Moena. Domenico was, no doubt, influenced by the various styles of the many churches he had worked on in Italy and in particular the church in his home town. But he had nothing as a guide other than his memory, what he could see in his mind's eye and the skill of his hands. He could do little about the barrel shape of the Nissen hut walls and so used his great imagination to transform what was there.

On each side of the chancel he painted what looked like angels with instruments but which have been called many things over the years in articles. Again, keen to use the correct term, Aidan Weston-Lewis at the National Gallery of Scotland, was contacted.

> I would describe the images on the side walls as music-making Angels. The lily accompanying one of them is associated with the Archangel Gabriel and the Annunciation, but in this context I think it is intended more as a symbol of purity.

In the centre of the ceiling Domenico painted a white dove, the symbol of peace, flying in a blue sky. Further along the ceiling he painted the four evangelists, to whom the Gospel accounts in the New Testament are attributed: Matthew, Mark, Luke and John. They are symbolised, respectively as a man with wings, a lion, a bull and an eagle.

Between all of these images Domenico painted the walls to look like stone. With his overall design he had to allow for the dormer windows that are situated one each side of the chancel. The other two windows are situated within what would later become the nave.

With the help of Patrick Sutherland Graeme, whose family included generations of clergy, a pair of curtains was ordered from a firm of church furnishers in Exeter, the money coming from the chapel fund. Despite the distance and German bombs, the curtains arrived at Lamb Holm and were hung either side of the altar, just as Domenico had intended.

Finding out which company supplied the curtains turned out to be one of the easiest pieces of research. Quite a few articles about the chapel have included the story of how money collected by Italians selling items they had made was used to purchase curtains from an Exeter firm specialising in church furnishings. The name is never given but it took only a few moments on the Internet to find J. Wippell & Company Ltd; Clerical outfitters, church furnishers and academic robe-makers since 1789, Exeter.

A letter to the company was responded to quickly by director Gerald Miller. Although the company had no record of such a sale, he confirmed that there has never been another firm of church furnishers in the city and so, if the curtains in the Orkney chapel had been supplied by an Exeter firm, then it was undoubtedly J. Wippell & Company. Eventually, the original curtains had to be replaced and the ones in the chapel today were made by John and Sheena Muir's daughter, Christine.

A carpenter made a tabernacle from the salvaged wood and this was put on the altar. Four candlesticks, two each of brass and wrought iron, were placed on top. This is exactly as the altar looks today, although photographs show that, at various times, all six candlesticks have been displayed and sometimes an altar cloth (a present from Maria Chiocchetti in 1964). Visitors occasionally leave messages within the tabernacle and these are removed and passed on to the local Catholic priest.

With the chancel virtually complete and services taking place regularly, the Italians thought that the beauty of what had been created made the remainder of the building look even uglier than it did before. The decision was taken to hold the now popular classes elsewhere and to line and paint the entire interior of the Nissen hut to make a proper nave.

This was a significant undertaking but Major Buckland helped to secure more wood, paid for out of the chapel fund, and a framework was subsequently made against the rest of the remaining inside walls. This time plasterboard was obtained, instead of the inferior pressed cardboard used for the chancel walls.

Domenico had intended to paint the whole of the 'nave' to look like brickwork. Such a task was too great for one man but Domenico was the only artist in Camp 60. However, his good friend Sergeant Giovanni Pennisi was still on nearby Burray, where regular services had been held for some time by Father Luigi Borsarelli in the chapel that had been built in Camp 34.

Major Buckland arranged for Pennisi to be freed of his duties and the two artists began work. Some accounts say that Pennisi travelled each day between camps to work alongside Domenico and he certainly appeared to still be in the Burray camp after the Italians on Lamb Holm had left, so this version may be accurate. Like Domenico, Buttapasta, Palumbi and a few others, Pennisi was allowed to work full-time on the chapel, his work on the barriers covered by others.

The chapel became many things to the men in Camp 60. It was a focus; an escape to cultural and spiritual freedom while their bodies remained in captivity. Men thrown together in such unnatural circumstances could not be expected to eat, sleep and work side by side without some conflict, but the chapel brought them together in a way that no band, theatre or football team could ever achieve. It was a link to loved ones back home, who would be praying in their own little chapels.

The walls of what would become the nave were lined with plasterboard and a dado added at the same point at which the lower section of the rood screen was attached to the wall. The camp's carpenters had built an additional wooden framework, which allowed plasterboard to be fixed so that the wall beneath the dado was horizontal, in contrast to the barrel shape of the rest of the room.

Above the dado Domenico and Pennisi painted hundreds of grey-coloured bricks, which must have been a test of patience as well as skill. The bricks cover the whole of the ceiling, for the entire length of the nave.

Below the dado they painted the plasterboard to look like stone, with the grisaille panels continuing the theme of those in the chancel, although without the wheat and grapes. From a distance the panels appear as though they are real carved stone. Like so much of the interior, the walls, whether curved or flat, give the three-dimensional illusion of a depth that is not actually there. They also painted the four dormer windows to look like stained glass. Pennisi painted much of the wall at the west end, incorporating the letters 'IHS' above the door, reflecting the letters painted under the altar and within one of the gates of the rood screen.

There were two electricians in Camp 60, Michele De Vitto and Assunto Micheloni. They ran a cable from the roof of the nearest hut to the top of the chapel and hung lights from the ceiling so that the craftsmen could work — and men could pray — at any time of the day or night. Later on they put lights in the vestry to illuminate the glass upon which the figures of St Francis of Assisi and St Catherine of Siena were painted, so that people standing in the nave could see the saints lit up from behind.

This photograph of a Camp 60 work party shows electrician Michele De Vitto standing second from the left. *Photograph by James W. Sinclair.*

Micheloni's family were not traced. However, Margaret De Vitto, the widow of Michele De Vitto, still lives in Lancashire and she told about her husband's life leading up to and after his stay in Camp 60.

Michele was born in January 1921 in Ariano Irpino, near Naples. He left school at the age of fourteen and an electrician in the village took him under his wing, which is how he gained his apprenticeship. However, he was called up at eighteen and sent to do his army training in northern Italy.

He was later caught up in the North African campaigns, fighting Montgomery, and it was during this time that he was taken prisoner. Michele was one of a large group of captured Italians who were subsequently packed on to a ship 'like sardines'. In an effort to avoid German U-Boats, the ship sailed for Britain taking a route that went via South America. Eventually, they landed at Liverpool and were later transported to Orkney. He was sent to Camp 60.

To be honest he seemed to have been quite happy there! Because he was skilled he was given a lot of freedom and worked alongside a British electrician on the cableways and the cranes, really anything electrical that needed repairing. Michele had no fear of heights and would often be the one who climbed up a mast to carry out a potentially dangerous job. There was a radio in the camp that was linked to speakers around the compound and Michele often had to tune this. The men came from all over Italy and they were always asking him to find a station that was from their home area.

Michele said the chapel that was being built meant a great deal to the Italians. It was a place where men could sit quietly and pray. He sometimes talked about how they used every possible opportunity to gather materials to use in its creation and in particular he remembered when they fitted the bell in the bell tower.

In September 1944, Michele De Vitto arrived in Skipton along with the other men from the camp. They found Overdale camp rather bleak, like an early version of Camp 60, so the Italians started to transform their new home as they had done once before. Margaret explained:

Michele helped out at a local electrical company and travelled around the town carrying out small repairs. He even sorted out the lighting for the stage at the town hall. Like many of the young people in the area my friends and I attended the local ceilidhs, which were held at the church hall. The Italians were not allowed to enter but would often stand around outside on the other side of the fence, just to listen to the music. At the end of the night, several of us used to chat to them through the railings, and that was how I met Michele.

The jobs he did in town didn't fill all his time and he also had to work on the land. Michele ended up with a group of Land Army girls at a nearby farm. One day he was working on a tractor when someone mistakenly turned on the power and the engine burst into life. Michele's hand was badly injured, with the result that he lost two fingers, which finished his career as an electrician. This effectively meant he was no longer a skilled man and, as a consequence, was repatriated early on.

It was a difficult period. His mother and father were in Italy, but I was in England and my parents would not let me travel to Italy at that time. The enormous amount of red tape that had to be waded through by Italians wishing to come back to Britain meant that it was two years before Michele was able to return to Skipton.

If, within six months, Michele and I had not married and he had not found a job then he would have been forcibly sent back to Italy. He had to keep in regular contact with the local police station for several years, even though the police sergeant lived a few doors away!

We married two months after his return and my family helped him to obtain employment at a local garage. Later, we moved to Earby in Lancashire and Michele found a job with a plastics manufacturer. For a short while he tried to make a better living in Canada, where one of his brothers had moved after the war, but I was pregnant and couldn't join him, so he returned to Britain. The plastics company was keen to have him back and he stayed with them until he retired.

Michele De Vitto died in 2007 at the age of eighty-seven. He left behind three children, eight grandchildren and four great grandchildren . . . and a chapel, on a tiny, windswept, Orcadian island.

By the spring of 1944, work on the causeways had been forging ahead for several months. Following plans formulated after the research carried out by the university professors, the Blondins had been used to drop five-ton concrete blocks in a pell-mell fashion to form an outer layer for the bolsters, right up to low-water level. Heavier blocks could have been carried by the cableways, but suddenly releasing more than this weight posed too great a risk of tangling wires.

Above the water level a layer of ten-ton 'clothing blocks' were laid carefully by a crane, which moved slowly along the surface of the causeway. When this had been sufficiently levelled out a narrow gauge track could be laid, which allowed blocks to be transported by train from the block-making yard to whatever position the crane had reached.

June 1944. Not a sight likely to be seen again; a train (named the *Winston Churchill*) crossing Water Sound causeway between South Ronaldsay and Burray. *Source: Balfour Beatty.*

The Balfour Beatty engineers had devised an innovative scissor-release mechanism that enabled the operator of the Blondins or the crane to detach the block at whatever point they wanted. This meant they could be laid to a carefully worked out pattern, which may not be that obvious, driving over the causeways today.

There were five block-making yards, one on Lamb Holm and two each on Burray and mainland Orkney. The scarcity of water meant that several used seawater, along with local sand. Between them the yards turned out concrete blocks at a staggering rate of 300 a day, which was just as well as more than 66,000 were required by the time all four structures were complete.

Orcadian Alf Hutcheon started work in the Rockworks blockyard in 1943, at the age of fourteen.

I joined Balfour Beatty straight from school and within a very short time was given the job of train driver! The train only had one gear to go forwards and one for reverse. It would pull wagons along, stopping at specific points where each skip would in turn have added sand, cement, crushed rock and 'dust', i.e. the remains of what was left when the stones had been crushed into chips.

The lot would be tipped into a mixer with water and then poured into the moulds to make concrete blocks. They had to be left for several days to cure before they could be used on the barriers.

The Balfour Beatty men came from all over Britain and were paid well, being on piecework (earning more as productivity increased). There were a few of us young lads and we worked hard, but at the end of our first week we saw that we had not been given the extra money for the additional output. When we complained we were told that we were too young, so the following week we worked slowly . . . the extra money soon came our way. It meant that I was on five pounds a week while my father, who was driving a van at that time, earned two pounds ten shillings.

The Italians were already working at the blockyard when I joined. The Rockworks yard was on the south side of mainland Orkney, which meant that the POWs had to travel over by boat each day from Lamb Holm. They hated the cold and built themselves a shelter that they would dash into whenever there was a flake of snow. They often had a small fire going in their shelter and one day an Italian threw on a bottle of what he thought was paraffin — only it was petrol! They all rushed outside with their faces blackened.

By 1944, Balfour Beatty estimated it had sufficient blocks for the barriers and Alf Hutcheon was laid off. He worked for a while as a projectionist at the Strond cinema in St Mary's, where the Italians were sometimes allowed to visit, but later trained as a mechanic.

12
The Façade

While the inside of the chapel became ever more elaborate and befitting its purpose, the outside, in particular the entrance, did nothing to convey what would be found on entering. The decision was made to create a façade, but such a creation would have to do more than simply hide the ugly frontage of a Nissen hut; it had to equal the craftsmanship of what had been achieved inside. It had to invite the passer-by to enter.

The façade was designed not by Domenico but by Pennisi, and this was where the stonemason Buttapasta proved his worth. He picked his team and work commenced. The men dug a hole at the front of the hut to create foundations, while the carpenters built various wooden moulds so that concrete blocks could be made and later assembled to match the design made by Pennisi. In many ways it was exactly like making five-ton blocks to drop into the sea, except on a smaller scale and with the need for different shapes.

Pennisi designed the façade to incorporate two lancet windows, either side of the door, and so the bricklayers — quite probably Barcaglioni and Battiato — altered the existing brickwork to match the shape and size of the intended openings. One of the carpenters set to work, making the wooden window frames.

A buttress was built at either side of the façade to add strength and balance. Each one was capped with a four-sided pinnacle. The gable is decorated with cusps, which are repeated on the bell tower and the portico pediment.

Pennisi moulded the cusp and pinnacle out of clay, which enabled him to make a plaster-of-Paris cast so that concrete replicas could be produced in the quantities required. He used the same method to create the blind arching that is fixed to the face of the façade and around the buttresses. This was painted subsequently in a terracotta colour, making it contrast sharply with the rest of the façade, which was painted white.

The façade incorporates many different influences and styles, from the rather Gothic cusps to the more classical portico, but the overall effect is one of harmony and balance. Above the entrance, in the tympanum, is Pennisi's bas-relief head of Christ. It is one of the most striking elements of the whole façade and has been made with great skill. Pennisi succeeded in capturing an expression that could be interpreted in many different ways, depending upon the person viewing it.

The bas-relief head is generally thought to be made of red clay that has been fired, but the head, like so much of the chapel, is made of cement. In this case it has been coloured red. Does that take anything away from this miniature work of art? No. When you consider the limitations under which the Italians worked, every tiny creation is an incredible achievement. If the results of the

Italian POWs praying during the summer of 1944. *Photograph by James W. Sinclair.*

efforts of one man, working with such a 'base' material more than sixty-five years ago can, today, make us stare in wonder, then Pennisi is connecting with people long after his death in a way that many people find difficult even when they are alive.

Buttapasta fitted the floor of the entrance with inlaid stone, carefully cut and polished to read '1944' in Roman numerals. The carpenters added the arched windows on either side of the door and these were painted to look like stained glass, just as the dormer windows had been.

At the top of the main gable the Italians built a small bell tower, although they had no bell to put in it until shortly before they left Lamb Holm. They fitted it with a wooden headstock and attached a rope that would enable a bell to be rung from just inside the door, when one could be found. On top of this belfry they fixed a cross made out of wrought iron.

While the rood screen and nave were being completed inside the chapel and the façade was being worked on outside, dramatic events were taking place in Italy and throughout mainland Europe. By the end of May, the Germans had retreated from Anzio and Rome was liberated shortly afterwards. On 6th June more than 130,000 Allied troops landed on five Normandy beaches. Operation Overlord, now known more commonly as the D-Day landings, had begun.

The living conditions for the Italians in Orkney continued to change. When not working, they could travel up to a distance of five miles from the camp, but they had to be within the perimeter by ten o'clock at night. The fence around Camp 60 had not yet been removed (and was not until the camp was taken down). They were still not allowed to visit public houses or places of entertainment or to form relationships with women. The latter was impossible to enforce rigidly, and throughout the country many romances blossomed between Italians and local women, often resulting in marriage after the war had ended.

During the summer, Padre Giacomo wrote an account of the creation of the chapel for the POW newspaper *Il Corriere del Sabato*. The following is a translation of the published article.*

* OA Ref D31/27/4

Skerry Sound, looking towards Lamb Holm. At the far end are the blockships *Lycia* and *Ilsenstein*. Source: *Orkney Library Archives*.

I was sent to Camp 60 to minister to the religious needs of my prisoner compatriots, arriving there on 30th September 1943. The first thing that occurred to me was that there should be a church where the brave soldiers of Italy could gather around the altar of God for communal prayer. The difficulty was to find suitable premises, a by no means simple matter owing to the layout of the camp.

The difficulty was, however, overcome and work began about the middle of November, although the season was not the most favourable. The church is now an accomplished fact, and stands as an object of real beauty and a source of joy to myself and the prisoners, who watch it daily growing richer in decoration and embellishments created out of the Italian genius for delicate taste and religious sensibility, and executed with true artistic skill.

What of the inauguration? The date is not yet fixed, neither is the exact form of the Dedication Ceremony, which will have to be organised meticulously down to the last detail.

I am able to give the readers of *Il Corriere del Sabato* some details of the work accomplished under the guidance of the painter Chiocchetti, an artist of great talent, who, besides undertaking personally the pictorial and decorative part of it, also drew all plans, drawings and designs for the construction of the altar, altar rails, flooring, tabernacle, candlesticks, lamps, windows and coloured glass, plus all the details for the ornamental woodwork.

I should say that in its *tout ensemble*, as in detail, the church at Camp 60 is second to none in all the POW camps located in various parts of Great Britain.

Chaste and aesthetic in style, in complete harmony with the best conceptions of religious art, the church of Camp 60 is dedicated to The Madonna under the title of 'Regina Pacis' (Queen of Peace). The gentle likeness of the Blessed Virgin, bearing in her arms the Holy Infant Jesus, offering his Mother an olive branch — symbol of peace — occupies the central portion of the reredos. She is encircled by a cordon of lovely cherubim who bear a scroll inscribed, *'Regina Pacis ora pro Nobis'* (Queen of Peace Pray for us); the invocation and prayer of suffering humanity pleading with the mother of God for peace, work and tranquillity.

On either side of the Blessed Virgin are two pictures, painted on glass, of the two holy, special patron saints of Italy: St Francis of Assisi and St Catherine of Siena. The vault carries the symbols of the four evangelists: St Matthew, St Mark, St John and St Luke, and lower down on either side are frescoed two cherubim and two seraphim with their instruments playing celestial harmonies. In the centre of the vault, high above all, hovers the white dove shedding its radiance, symbol of the Holy Spirit, the light, guide and strength of the Church and of all the faithful.

This is all the work of Chiocchetti, who, we may say in passing, is already known by his other, much admired, works of art both in, and outside, the camp; notably his Christmas 'Bethlehem' which was much loved and admired in the church and is still on view to visitors in a special room. It is a praiseworthy masterpiece in decorated plastic.

The assistants and craftsmen who are responsible for the construction of the altar, rails, candelabra, lamps, woodwork, lighting etc. are as follows: D. Buttapasta, P. Barcaglioni, S. Battiato, A. Sforza, Micheloni, Primavera, Palumbi, De Vitto and others, who, under the guidance of Chiocchetti cooperated skilfully in the creation of this beautiful church.

When all is completed and the inauguration has taken place, photographs will be sent to the *Corriere*. These will show readers that this matter has been taken very seriously in Camp 60.

This new church rises beside many others, erected with praiseworthy religious zeal and sacred aspirations. Whatever their sad or happy situation, the Italians love to see arise a temple that shall proclaim their faith in Christ, their religious traditions and their thousand-year-old civilization.

And now that the essential part of the work is nearing completion, it is incumbent upon me to emphasise to the readers that, without the support and personal interest of the camp commander, Major T. P. Buckland, which enabled all difficulties of space, premises, material and means to be surmounted, this little church could have remained nothing but a beautiful dream.

With a minimum of resources and in spite of many hindrances, inevitable under existing circumstances, a beautiful little masterpiece has emerged, visited and admired with delight by many British visitors, to say nothing of the prisoners of war in the camp themselves.

Recognition of his service must also be paid to Sergeant Major Fornasier, of the Italian Tank Corps, who grudged no effort to ensure that the little church should arise to the spiritual comfort of the prisoners and the worthy performance of religious functions.

'Where there's a will, there's a way' (all is possible to the determined).

So it has come about, and I through the medium of the *Corriere*, grateful and deeply moved, feel that I must thank the camp commandant, the Italian camp leader, the artist, the collaborators and all the prisoners, for having not only fulfilled my hopes, but for having surpassed them.

Military Chaplain
Father G. Giacobazzi
Order of the Little Brothers

13
Summer, Sport and Shipwreck

One of the most amusing stories is that of Primiano Malvolti in Camp 34. He was a close friend of Gino Caprara, who narrated the following tale about the first sports event held in Camp 34.

For nearly two years Primiano belonged to the staff and was exonerated from doing heavy work because the doctors declared he had a serious problem with his right leg. As a matter of fact, he always walked leaning on a knotty stick. For that reason he was very popular. Humorously, the British soldiers and sentries had nicknamed him 'Shipwreck'.

Well, on the day we had our athletic competitions, all of us were surprised to see that Shipwreck was entering on to the field to compete with the others. In short, he excelled in several sports — one-hundred yards, long jump, throwing the javelin, discus and hammer-throwing. Obviously, at the end of every game he was always among those who were called to their prize. Also, he was awarded with the only cup to be given to the best athlete in the sports ground!

Mr Gordon Nicol was in charge, granting prizes to the winners, so at the end of every competition Malvolti's name was in the air. Everyone present shouted out and laughed. Even the commanding officer (very earnestly) congratulated him.

But as soon as we got back to our huts, the British NCO came in and

Gordon Nicol presenting first prize for the high jump to Coriolano 'Gino' Caprara. *Source: Orkney Library Archives. Photograph by James W. Sinclair.*

shouted: 'Shipwreck, to the Commandant.' Malvolti, very reluctantly, got up. Resigned, and with a deep sigh, he said, 'Gosh, I knew it!'

Primiano told us what happened when he was introduced to the Commandant. The NCO knocked at the door and announced, 'Malvolti's here, Sir.' The answer was, 'Come in'. Primiano went in, saluted and stood. The commanding officer didn't say a word and dismissed Malvolti, handing him a card with only one word printed on it. It was 'Quarry'.

We all had a big laugh and told Malvolti the British officer had been too good to him and he was lucky not to have been in a German POW camp!

Asked later if he knew that his friend was faking his injury, Gino replied:

Of course! Being my closest friend I was aware that he was as sound as a bell. But what amazed all of us (including our sentries and the British commanding officer) was how he could have deceived the doctors. He did not like to work on the barriers and suffer cold and bad weather and for that reason he walked lame, making fun of everybody for nearly two years. By our comrades he was considered a hero and foolish at the same time. But at the end he was betrayed by his passion for sports and was commanded to do the heaviest work in the quarry. 'Better late than never,' the others said.

A particularly large sports day, involving both camps, was held on Lamb Holm during July. As was to be expected the event was planned like a military operation. The events ranged from the javelin and discus to the one-hundred-yards dash and the four-by-four-hundred-yards relay.

All work stopped. Construction workers, Orkney families and other civilians were invited and the event took on a carnival atmosphere as, for one day, people tried to forget that about half the world was at war. Stalls were set up and the crowd was entertained by a variety of acrobatics, clowns and music from both camp bands.

A report on the day's events was later published in the 19th August issue of *Il Corriere del Sabato*. Peter MacDonald gave permission to reproduce the translation of the article that appears in his father's book, *Churchill's Prisoners*, under the headline 'News From The Camps — Sports Day at 60'.

In the presence of the whole of Camp 60 with a large representation from Camp 34, led by W. O. Bertoni, together with many British civilian and military personnel, including the commanding officer and all the officers on the bunting-dressed podium, the Sports Day of Camp 60 took place on the sports field at Lamb Holm on 16th July.

At 14:00 precisely the four athletic teams — Sparvieri, Ardente, Limatori and Disperata — under the overall direction of Sgt Rizzato . . . the sports instructor, marched out in front of the crowded stands and the brightly coloured crowds to enthusiastic applause.

The clear and kindly sky allowed the competition to follow a perfect timetable and gave every opportunity for taking photographs.

The highest placed team was Ardente, showing superiority in every

Sports Day, July 1944. The shot put. In the distance is the podium for the British officers. *Photograph by James W. Sinclair.*

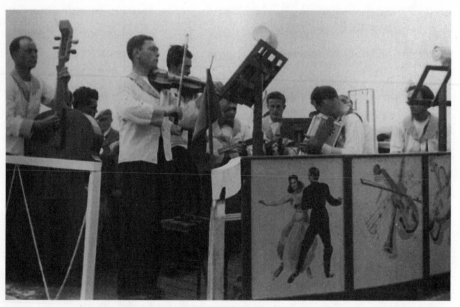

The band dressed up for the big sports day on Lamb Holm. *Photograph by James W. Sinclair.*

event, taking first place in the 100m* flat race with Marinucci and Meozzi, in the 4 x 100m relay with the quartet of Perazzolo, Marinucci, Silvertri and Meozzi, in the long jump with Perazzolo and the high jump with the skilful Pilo, and taking second places in the 200m flat and javelin, demonstrating both ability and technique.

The team placed second was Limatori, under their captain Bruno Volpi, which, although not coming first in many events, held most of the second places, but also showed definitive ability in the 800m flat race with the unbeatable Gambacorta.

In third place was Disperata, captained by Brecevich, which took first place in the throwing events with Brecevich in the discus, Altinier in the javelin and Catelani in the weight.

In last place was Sparvieri, captained by Di Fiore, which, if not very highly placed, were still first in the 80m obstacle race with Di Fiore. The competition between the teams ensured a great struggle in the events with the athletes once again showing the virtues of their race, seizing both the attention and the admiration of the great crowd of spectators who repeatedly broke out into enthusiastic applause.

During the intervals the orchestra on its radiant podium played most movingly items of dance and light music. The comic Mezzacapo and his assistants provoked much hilarity from spectators with his magnesium flash lamp, especially from the fairer sex.

Following the main events were the more humorous games: three-legged and wheelbarrow races, egg and spoon races, sack races and so on, causing sides to split with laughter.

Mention must also be made of the game of football for the not-so-young, in which the Rossi beat the Verdi by two goals to nil, demonstrating the speed of snails, internal pains and feet in the air, arousing healthy laughter from the spectators.

The day reached its epilogue with the presentations of the prizes by Mr G. G. Nicol . . . who cordially congratulated every single one of the champions.

* As this article was written originally in Italian the distances are given in metric.

Sports Day, July 1944. The winners. *Source: Orkney Library Archives. Photograph by James W. Sinclair.*

The magnificence of the prizes was due to the indefatigable activities of Major Buckland and Sergeant Major Fornasier to find them, and to whom we offer our grateful thanks.

The happy success of the day is to the honour of all concerned and in particular to those who worked so hard on the equipment and the organisation, amongst who were the intrepid and active Cesare Cerica and Captain Buonasera Acri and all the submariners.*

Also to be complimented is the jury, composed of Sergeants Rizzato and Vissani and Captains Acri, Bombaci, Celin, Casini and the super athlete Ripamonti for their correctness and impartiality. All the members of Camp 60 will retain memories of this grand day, the aspects of which will be remembered by those with various photographs of the events.

* *The POWs included the crew from an Italian submarine.*

Just how far the Italians were becoming integrated, and trusted, is demonstrated by an amusing story about a group who, while one day walking past the Burray pier at high tide, spotted a conger eel. The eel, about three feet long, caused great excitement amongst the men, who asked the nearby guard if they could borrow his rifle and bayonet! This was duly handed over but, despite all their best efforts, the eel could not be speared. Apparently, the local baker captured it later on that day.

There is no record of whether the eel ended up on the menu. In addition to fish, the men sometimes caught other local wildlife. One inmate acquired a ferret from a local farmer and used this to hunt rabbits. The skins of captured animals were given to the farmer and the meat kept for the camp kitchen.

Following the D-Day landings in June, the eyes of the world were focused on mainland Europe, where major events were occurring almost daily. Shortly after the liberation of Rome, Badoglio was replaced as Prime Minister by Invanoe Bonomi in a move to unite Italy against Mussolini, who had set up a puppet government under the control of Hitler.

No one gave much thought to small Orkney islands. The threat to Scapa Flow was considered to be greatly reduced and, during 1944, the defences around the harbour were scaled down significantly. Men and equipment were sent to the south of England where their need was much greater.

Several of the gun emplacements had become empty concrete structures, visited only by gulls. Even the balloon barrage, which had so often been a part of the harbour's skyline, was moved to London to provide greater protection for the capital.

By the summer the barriers were virtually complete and most of the Balfour Beatty construction workers left Orkney. This led to the disbandment of the 2nd Orkney Battalion of the Home Guard, known locally as 'Orkney's Foreign Legion' because it contained so many civilians from the south. Pockets of normality began to return. Buildings were returned to civilian use and hotels in Kirkwall were once more open to the public.

Increasingly, the Italians in Camp 60 were being sent to help out on local farms as their work on the barriers grew less. Even the tarmac surface of the causeways was to be laid by Orkney council workers, not by the Italians. But as late as the summer of 1944, new Italians still arrived at Camp 60. One of these was Roberto Pendini, who made his first return trip to Lamb Holm in May 2008.

I was in the fifth infantry regiment of the Agrigento division and was captured by the Americans on 20th July 1943 during the battle of Santo Stefano in Sicily. I was an expert in quarrying and mining so was transferred to a marble quarry in the San Pellegrino mountains in Palermo. The material we extracted was used in the construction of airfield landing strips.

After the D-Day landings I was handed over into the keeping of the British army and my journey to Orkney began. Via a small ship, I sailed from Palermo to Algeria and then onwards to Glasgow in the 50,000-ton *Orion London*. There were fifty Italians in the group and we were escorted by four British soldiers. From Glasgow we sailed in yet another ship and upon our arrival we were split between Camp 60 and Camp 34.

I ended up in Lamb Holm. We were young and the older men in Camp 60 called us 'Mussolini's Balilla' [meaning they were Mussolini's boys, the Italian version of the Hitler Youth]. However, they welcomed us well. Many of us considered the British to be friends, not enemies. By this stage the Italians were allowed to go out and mix with local families, and I remember they were very kind and tolerant towards us.

In the evenings we could sit in the canteen, which provided hot drinks, as well as a range of items such as toothpaste, shaving gear, soap, shoelaces and shoe polish.

The chapel was obviously at an advanced stage by the time Roberto Pendini arrived and he says that it was very well used, with all of the men attending mass on a Sunday.

The conversion of the two Nissen huts into what can be seen today was a process of different projects. As the chancel became increasingly ornate, so the rood screen was started and while this progressed it was then decided to convert the whole of the inside. With the façade underway, there was only one part of the building that had not been touched — the roof.

The craftsmen could see that the weakest point of the chapel would be the ability of the sections of corrugated iron sheets to keep out damp over any length of time, particularly if there was no maintenance being carried out. If water was to get into the building their great works of art would be destroyed.

They decided to cover the entire roof with bolster netting and then apply a layer of sand and cement. This was a messy process but it didn't require skill. When it was dry the mixture would be lighter and carry its own weight but when applied it was a wet, heavy mass. Eventually, the roof was covered and the building, with its valuable contents, had a strong concrete coating on top of the original sheets of corrugated iron. It was the best that could be done.

It was around this time that Major Buckland decided he wanted a photograph taken of the chapel with the craftsmen who had built it, and this decision led to two of the most famous photographs ever taken of the chapel.

James W. Sinclair was one of Orkney's best-known photographers. He was the only civilian on the islands during the war with a permit from the military to take outdoor pictures. As such, he was the official photographer for the two Italian camps and had been invited to several occasions, such as sports events. It is almost certainly his work when black and white images — showing Italians standing around the statue of St George on the parade ground, playing billiards or bowls — are reproduced in articles about the Orkney camps.

When the chapel was virtually complete, Major Buckland invited the photographer back once again, this time to capture on film the men who had been mainly responsible for the chapel's creation. However, the bell tower at this point was still empty and as Domenico and Giuseppe were lined up either side of the entrance, a comment about the absence of a bell suddenly had the two craftsmen running off, much to the surprise of the photographer and the British officer.

The two Italians quickly returned carrying a ladder and a piece of cardboard,

Chiocchetti (left) with Palumbi, late summer 1944. *Source: Orkney Library Archives. Photograph by James W. Sinclair.*

cleverly cut to look like a bell. When the 'bell' was fixed in place, no one would know by looking at a photograph that it was not real. Later, James Sinclair took a shot of twenty-four men, the main Italians who worked on the chapel.

One of the most unsuccessful pieces of research was trying to discover the origin of the bell that was hung subsequently in the bell tower. Where there are references to it in articles, they invariably state that the bell came from a blockship. This may be the case, but the ships sunk to block the sounds are fairly well documented and nothing was found that said one was called *SD Accord* — the eight-inch high bell is inscribed: *SD Accord, Aberdeen, 1918*. The 'blockship theory' felt a little too convenient.

Probably the most famous photograph ever taken of the chapel, showing twenty-four of the men who helped to build it. The paint on the lancet windows is clearly visible. *Source: Orkney Library Archives. Photograph by James W. Sinclair.*

Initially, it seemed to be relatively easy to find out more about the bell's history, but enquiries with the National Maritime Museum, Aberdeen City Archives and the Aberdeen Maritime Museum drew a blank. There is no listing for such a vessel in either *Lloyds Register* or *Mercantile Marine List* for 1918 or 1919. The origins of the bell remain a mystery.

The ability to reach mainland Orkney by simply walking across barrier number one resulted increasingly in groups of men being sent to supplement the scarce local labour. They often worked at the Kirkwall dockyards, unloading cargoes from the holds of ships. One day a group of women at the R. Garden Ltd lemonade factory took pity on the passing Italians, who were covered in dust and grey powder from working in the hold of a ship and the women later made them masks to cover their mouths and noses.

When they had completed their tasks the Italians could have the bizarre experience of drinking coffee in the Italian-run Central Café! Livio Zanre had

Livio Zanre ran the Central Café in Kirkwall during the time that the Italians were in Camp 60. *Source: Orkney Library Archives.*

arrived in Orkney in the early 1930s and, after working in the ice cream business, he set up his own café, which became quite popular.

Unfortunately, like many Italians living in Britain at the time, he had not acquired British citizenship. When Italy entered the war on the side of Germany he was interned like so many others, following Winston Churchill's order to 'collar the lot'. In Livio Zanre's case this meant the Isle of Man, a place where large numbers of Italians, including whole families, were locked up.

He was released when Italy capitulated and, by the summer of 1944, was once more serving in his little Kirkwall café. But having groups of his fellow countrymen as guests must have been an extraordinary experience. Apparently, he never forgave the authorities for what they did and a few years after the war he sold up and moved back to Italy.

14
Farewell to Lamb Holm

Most articles about Camp 60 put the date of the departure of the Italians as the spring of 1945. However, there were some notable exceptions which claimed the date was September 1944. This includes a speech made by Bruno Volpi in 1995, on the fiftieth anniversary of the official opening of the Churchill Barriers, and also James MacDonald's book *Churchill's Prisoners*. The September date seemed the most likely as the Italians were only in Orkney to help build the barriers, which were virtually complete by the summer of 1944.

Granted, they helped out on local farms as the work on the barriers tailed off, but it seemed unlikely that such a huge workforce would have been kept in Orkney when the labour shortage in England was desperate. However, there was no evidence to prove one date or the other. Even the Orkney library was stumped on this, replying that most people had assumed it was 1945 but, upon checking archive information, there was nothing to confirm this. Sheena Wenham was contacted to see if her aunt, Alison, could remember when the Italians left Lamb Holm.

Sheena was later able to confirm that the time and date written in her aunt's diary for the departure of the Italians in Camp 60 was one o'clock, 9th September 1944. She and her father had met them to say goodbye. Was this sufficient proof? Fiona Zeyfert was asked if she would be willing to try to obtain her grandfather's army service records. Some while later a large envelope arrived in the post, containing the army records of Lt Colonel Buckland, along with his earlier seaman's records and a rather revealing document from the POW Inspector of Camps.

The army records confirmed that the Italians left Camp 60 on 9th September 1944, and were transferred to Overdale Camp near Skipton in Yorkshire.

The men in Camp 60 packed into the chapel for their last service. It was, of course, taken by Padre Giacomo. Someone had acquired a wind-up gramophone which was placed in the vestry and the service was conducted to the sound of the bells and choir of St Peter's in Rome. As it turned out, the chapel had been in use for only a short while, but the hope it had given the Italians while it was being built had made a very important contribution to their well-being.

Their departure could hardly have been more different from their arrival and many were sad at leaving behind the friends they had made of local Orkney families. They had walked on to Lamb Holm in the harsh winter of 1942 as enemies and many must have dreaded what these strange islands held in store for them.

Uniforms were cleaned, shoes were polished and hair was cut in preparation for their departure day. As they marched out of the gates of Camp 60 for the last time they did so with pride. Building the Churchill Barriers had taken four years and consumed more than 900,000 tons of concrete and rock. It had required vast amounts of equipment and materials and presented huge logistical and physical challenges. Men had been injured and men had died building them, but the construction workers and the Italians had worked side by side to defy many who said the project could never be achieved.

The Italians crossed barrier number one to St Mary's, where buses were waiting. Several people had gathered to say their goodbyes. As well as Patrick and Alison Sutherland Graeme, there were Balfour Beatty representatives and local families. Speeches were given, gifts and addresses exchanged as well as more than one promise to write, once men had returned safely home.

'The Italians presented my grandfather with a valedictory address thanking him for making their time in Orkney more bearable,' said Sheena Wenham. 'He was very proud of this and, in turn, promised the Italians that their chapel would never be demolished.'

The buses transported the Italians to Stromness, where they boarded a ship that took them on their second journey across the Pentland Firth. They landed without incident at Scrabster harbour and walked the short distance to Thurso railway station, where a train waited to take them to Yorkshire. The sixty men based near Stromness continued with their work in the dockyards.

In Camp 60 one Italian had not left. Domenico had been given permission to remain behind with the group of British soldiers who were given the task of dismantling and removing equipment and materials that could be used elsewhere, such as the kitchen ranges, bedding and furniture. Camp 60's deputy camp commander, Major Booth, was in charge of the small detachment of men.

Domenico's task was to complete the holy water stoup. It was the one item in the chapel that had not been finished and even though the Italians had gone and no one knew for certain what would happen to the building, Major Buckland had agreed that the artist could stay behind. Dismantling the camp was expected to take about ten days.

It was a surreal time for Domenico. With the departure of the men, the camp changed completely in one morning. There were no groups of Italians shouting and laughing, no musicians playing or people singing, no noisy card games. There was no queue for the showers and his footsteps echoed loudly as he walked up and down the wash block, with the choice of any sink. He was suddenly the only resident in the hut he had shared with other men for the last two and a half years. At night it was silent apart from the noise of the wind and creaking of the building.

Domenico was well known to the British soldiers and busied himself while they worked in the camp. He had designed the holy water stoup to be constructed in three sections so that the bowl, stand and base could be cemented together afterwards. The bowl has three angel heads around the outside. To achieve the spiral effect of the stand he used a large spring, obtained from one of the workshops, to provide the correct shape and give additional strength.

As he worked quietly and methodically, following his own design, the soldiers rapidly began to stack the items that would be taken away by army lorries the following week. He worked in one of the huts so that the chapel, which had been cleaned from top to bottom for the service the previous Sunday, would not get dirty. When the holy water stoup was completed a couple of soldiers helped to carry it over to the chapel. It was placed just inside the door, where it can be seen to this day.

Domenico left Camp 60 with the soldiers and the lorries. The camp gates were closed and locked for the last time. One can imagine that Domenico looked back through the barbed-wire fence with mixed emotions. In less than twelve months, the Italians had created a beautiful chapel out of scraps of leftover cement and material that others considered had no value. The chapel had become the main focus for the camp's inhabitants and had helped to rescue men from the depths of despair.

What would happen to it now? At some point Lamb Holm would be handed back to its owner and no doubt the camp, with all its huts and fencing, would be removed. But who would look after the little chapel and the statue of St George slaying the dragon? Who would protect it from the fierce Orkney winters?

Domenico was on his way to rejoin his comrades in Yorkshire and one day they would return to their homes and families. But as he travelled across barrier number one, he must have thought of the chapel, so small and fragile amongst the much larger Nissen huts, and feared for its future. Patrick Sutherland Graeme and many local people had said they would try to protect the building, but for now they couldn't even get to it, locked behind its barbed-wire fence. Where the men had been held captive and the chapel had helped to set them free, now the chapel was a prisoner.

Not all of the men from Camp 60 were sent to the Skipton camp and Roberto Pendini, along with about ten other Italians, was transported from Orkney to Glasgow by ship and then by train to Luton. Roberto and two others were moved to Chardingleye Farm in Ware, Herts, which was growing sugar beet and wheat at that time.

> The three of us were given a small house to live in and we cooked and ate our meals there. We were treated very well. In our spare time we could travel up to five miles from the farm. Mr Edwardson, the farmer, paid us each week and he gave me a bike, which enabled me to get as far as the local cinema.

The Italians who had been POWs in Britain were given greater freedom as

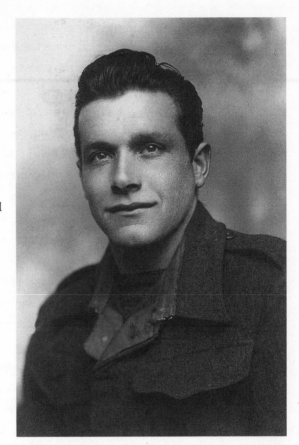

Roberto Pendini was one of several Italians who arrived at Camp 60 during the summer of 1944.

the summer of 1944 passed into autumn. This included access into shops, post offices and the cinema as well as being able to accept invitations into the homes of local people. Restrictions were later lifted on the use of public transport, although regulations preventing Italians from visiting pubs remained.

Shortly after the Italians had left Camp 60, Gordon Nicol sent a letter to his friend Major Buckland, which gives a good insight into the relationship between the two men and the challenges they faced in building the barriers and running the camp. From his comments it can be assumed that the small group of soldiers who had been left behind were still on Lamb Holm and that Camp 60 was now in a state of great disorder, which would have offended the British officer.

Dear Major Buckland,

Saturday morning and my first breather since last Sunday when I got back. So now I sit down in peace and quiet to write you, a pleasure I've been looking forward to for some time.

First please accept our thanks for the most delicious damsons. They were a great treat and a proportion found their way in due course under the pastry of a tart prepared by the lady of the house and enjoyed by her two colleagues. I'm afraid I kept on eating the ripest ones until the making of the tart and thoroughly enjoyed myself.

Then came your letter of farewell and the very nice memento of our sojourn in the Orkneys, an episode in our lives to which I will always look back with the greatest of pleasure. Will live in hope of a reunion at some not too distant date. I thank you.

One of my greatest regrets is that Mrs Buckland and the family were prevented by your sudden departure from seeing us all in our wonderful surroundings. Please convey to them these sentiments. I trust all are now restored to normal good health.

I was much relieved to hear that the doctors had found a reason for the pain you suffered in your chest and arm and hope you have followed it up by having treatment prescribed by someone who understands about such things.

Yesterday I went over the policies with Mr Graeme and you were much in my thoughts. I will refrain from describing the scene. You are best to remember it as you saw it last yourself.

This job has been one of four years of what seemed to be endless struggle, and then suddenly peace. I know we both enjoyed the times of 'endless struggle' better than the 'peace' and that is what I've found to be the case in all I've had to face in this short life. Once the goal has been reached, the eye automatically seeks another, just as we used to preach 'a completed camp is a retrograde camp'.

As I write, the sky is blue and little white horses caper about in the sunshine in front of the office. A feather of steam is over one of the boats at the pier, and beyond, the distant hills look friendly with lazy clouds high above them. You know it well!

On Wednesday I lunched with Mr & Mrs White and Miss Pease in the Murray Arms Hotel after a historic journey (for them). Robertson and his gang have now left and will return to take down the second carpet towards the end of next month.

As you know, one of the first things I did when approaching home after a visit to the capital was to see if all ten masts were standing. Now my task is easier as I don't have to count higher than seven. One leg of the V for victory sign on your lake island home is now missing and its mate will follow in a day or so. So far no consequences have arisen to justify detection of any of them. We have our own view about that as you know.

And now you are off to new adventures. Booth came in to say goodbye just before he left and gave me an indication of your whereabouts. I look forward to having some news from you when you have got settled into your permanent quarters.

I can imagine how you feel, and if you are fit again. I can visualise the changes that are about to take place in your environs.

I never cease to be grateful to the kind providence which guided your steps towards us. What condition the work would have been in today if your presence had been withheld I shudder to imagine, and I will always owe you a deep debt of gratitude for the forceful assistance you rendered to all who came in touch with you.

The little book you so kindly and thoughtfully sent me is but one more evidence of your thought for others, and will remain a very treasured possession reminding me as you so aptly put it 'of our prison days.'

I have one other souvenir from you which has meant a lot to me and that is the book on painting which you sent me and which guided me to my first success (?) with colour. This and your kindly encouragement, embarrassing at times when you brought the nobility to the studio, gave me the patience to persevere with what has turned out to be a pastime which is giving pleasure to others as well as to myself. I started a portrait of Mrs White yesterday and will probably spend the weekend to complete the good work.

Your own sits beside me as I write. I must finish it off and will send it over to you — if you wish to have it (or would the family object?)

I had a restful holiday but was delayed for two days on the return journey. Mrs Nicol asked me to send her best wishes and thanks when I write. She would not be pleased if she knew how long it has taken me to get started.

Once again please accept my thanks and good wishes. As the French put it — Bonne chance et bon courage.

Yours sincerely

G. G. Nicol

Domenico joined his comrades in Overdale camp. Most of the men worked on local farms although some apparently worked in a nearby chocolate factory. Domenico was asked to help create the scenery at the local theatre and ended up 'painting the main street of Skipton with its impressive church'.

He became very friendly with a man called David Harvey, who was responsible for the maintenance of electrical equipment at the camp. Domenico's friendship with Mr and Mrs Harvey lasted the whole of his life and it was a letter from them at the beginning of 1959 that first alerted the artist to the fact that the chapel still existed.

Amongst the men was Sergeant Major Fornasier. His daughter Gina explained what happened when they arrived.

The men went to Skipton in North Yorkshire and lived in a camp on Embassy Road, my father being one of them. They worked on farms and in garages in and around the town before being sent back to Italy. Quite a few returned to the area and lived their lives out there. My father was one of them and also a man called Benvenuto Altinier who went back to Skipton to the same garage he worked at when he was a prisoner. He brought his wife with him and eventually opened his own garage.

Back in Orkney, the military presence on the islands and in Scapa Flow continued to be scaled down, as it was clear that by this point in the war Germany had neither the inclination nor the resources to consider attacking and inhabiting Orkney as a means of invading Great Britain. By November the threat was considered to be so slight that the whole of Orkney's Home Guard was stood down.

Camp 34 had started its own monthly newsletter, *Sole d'Italia* (Italian Sun), in July 1944. *Sole d'Italia* contained a mixture of puzzles, poems and stories written by the Italians and was produced on a small duplicating machine in the administration office. Sergeant Giovanni Pennisi often drew illustrations for the cover.

Gino Caprara provided a copy of the front cover of the November issue. Francis Roberts translated the text to reveal some extremely surprising content.

There are many shots of camp bands but the players are rarely identified. Sitting on the left, playing the mandolin, is Chiocchetti. The accordionist is Sforza, who would later often play a harmonium in the chapel for mass. He was a carpenter who worked on the chapel. The man on the guitar is Santini. He wrote to Chiocchetti in the 1960s after seeing publicity about the artist in a magazine.
Photograph by James W. Sinclair.

PRISONERS OF WAR CAMPS

CAMP OF ISSUE

THREEPENCE

Nº 924762

3d.

AVAILABLE IN CAMP OF ISSUE ONLY

This bottle containing a crucifix was presented to Orcadian Bill Johnstone in return for the oil he gave the Italians for their hair.

The Italians were paid in camp tokens, which they could spend in the canteen.

Several Italians were gifted craftsmen and many items that they made can still be seen in Orkney.

Chiocchetti painted a white dove, the symbol of peace, in the centre of the chancel ceiling.

Sergeant Primavera used bully-beef tins to make the lanterns in the chancel.

Chiocchetti painted icons of the four Apostles.

Music-making angels adorn the sides of the chancel.

Chiocchetti's Madonna and Child.

It is only when the gates are opened that Palumbi's heart is revealed.

Like Chiocchetti, Palumbi was forced to adapt his work to suit the barrel shape of the Nissen hut.

The staff and guards of Camp 60. Major Buckland is sitting in the centre, between the two dogs. *Photograph by James W. Sinclair.*

When the chancel was almost complete, the men started to turn the rest of the hut into a nave.

The ceiling in the nave. Painting the nave was too much for one man so Chiocchetti's friend Pennisi, who lived in Camp 34, was allowed to work on the Lamb Holm chapel.

The chapel entrance faces west, into the camp and towards Scapa Flow.

Pennisi's bas-relief of the head of Christ sits just beneath the bell tower.

The stonemason Buttapasta inlaid the entrance with cut and polished stones to read '1944' in Roman numerals, the year the chapel was completed.

Chiocchetti's portrait of Gordon Nicol, who was Resident Superintending Civil Engineer for the Churchill Barriers from March 1942 until their completion.

Major Buckland ordered sports equipment for the Italians from Lumley's in Glasgow, which were suppliers to the armed forces.

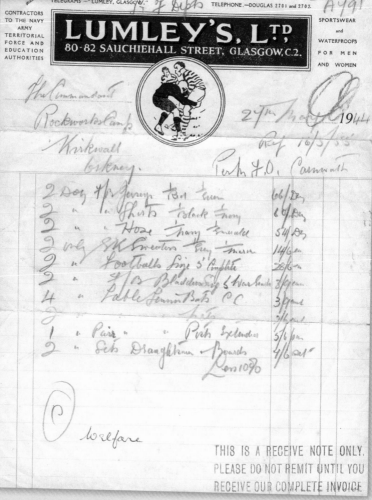

Chiocchetti in Skipton. He made friends with local man David Harvey. The person on the right is Micheloni, one of the two electricians from Camp 60.

In February 1946, Pizzi arrived in Naples on the same ship as Chiocchetti. He sent a telegram to tell his wife Nella that he would be home the next day. He had not seen her for nearly five years and Nella had heard no news of him for more than three. The message reads: 'Arrived at Naples. I'll soon be home. Kisses. Ugo.'

Caprara (left) with
two friends in
Lancashire, 1945,
wearing Italian
Labour Battalion
uniforms.

Skipton, 1945. Fornasier with
Leda, his future wife.

SUPERINTENDING CIVIL ENGINEER

(SPECIAL CONSTRUCTION),

ROCK WORKS,

KIRKWALL, ORKNEY.

Telephone No

Holm 217.

23ᵈ Sept 1944

Dear Major Buckland,

Saturday morning and my first breather since last Sunday when I got back. So now I sit down in peace and quiet to write you, a pleasure I've been looking forward to for some time.

First please accept our thanks for the most delicious damsons. They were a great treat and a profusion found their way in due course under the pastry of a tart prepared by the lady of the house and enjoyed by her two colleagues. I'm afraid I

The beginning of Gordon Nicol's letter to his friend Major Buckland shortly after the Italians had left Camp 60.

The Stations of the Cross were carved in Moena.

[12]

Eighty-nine-year-old Father Ronald Walls, Catholic priest in Orkney, October 2009. *Photograph by Anne Baxter.*

The Wayside Shrine has needed attention over the years to protect it from the weather.

Maria and Domenico Chiocchetti in April 1988.

The chapel built by Italian POWs in Letterkenny, Pennsylvania. *Photograph by David Goodman.*

About thirty miles from Nairobi, on the old road north-west of Limuru, is a tiny chapel built by Italian POWs who worked on the road. *Photograph by Molly Arbuthnott.*

The fresco of the Last Supper, painted by Mario Eugenio Ferlito in the Henllan chapel, West Wales. *Photograph by Molly Arbuthnott.*

The chapel in Hereford, West Texas. *Photograph courtesy of the* Hereford Brand *newspaper.*

Within the grounds of Camp Atterbury, Indiana, Italian POWs built this tiny chapel. *Photograph courtesy of Camp Atterbury Veteran's Memorial Museum.*

Roberto Pendini returned to Lamb Holm in 2008.
Photograph by Tom O'Brien, Vision Orkney Photographers.

Guido DeBonis in 2008 during his emotional return visit to see the chapel, the first time since he had left in 1944.

St George slaying the Dragon represents the 'will to "kill" all misunderstandings among people of different cultures'. (Bruno Volpi, Camp 60)

The translation is included here, but it is not the full article and is the reply of one man to an article that was in an earlier issue and apparently written by an Italian called Cipriani. How much the second writer's thoughts echo that of other men in the Burray camp is impossible to say.

I also feel, perhaps even more than you, a tightening of the heart when all too often I see the deserted chapel. But to tell the truth, from the time when this camp was established, those who attended the church never found the need to tread on each other's feet on account of the crowds! However, from a particular point in time, precisely from the landing in Sicily of the Allied Forces (10th July 1943), the religious observance has diminished considerably. I have tried to explain this, and I am not sure if my deliberations have hit the mark.

From the time of the Allied landing in Sicily, and even more so after the fall of Mussolini, the souls of the faithful have gone off the rails. Accustomed, as we were, in the belief of our inevitable victory, we could not adapt to the reality of the situation; it was as if our spirits had become suspended in between our past faith and present conditions, until, shaken out of our dream, we threw in the towel of our faith.

If things had rested there, the problems would have been minimal: but for us in Italy, religious faith had been instilled in us alongside faith in patriotism. We had, in certain cases, learned to believe in God in heaven and Mussolini on earth. It is not surprising, therefore, that along with the collapse of this latter faith, the other one which it sustained, should also collapse.

For others, and perhaps for the majority, the reason could be different. We expected a victory, not only of our armed forces, but also of our faith. The war which we were fighting was a holy war (or at least this is what we were told) against protestant England, against plutocratic, Judaic, Masonic democracies, against an atheist and communist Russia; victory was a right which, as Catholics, we expected (or so we were told or led to believe).

If, therefore, God does not help Catholics (as some might argue) what use is there in being religious?

Responding to all these points would take too long; I shall limit myself to a few observations. Is our Catholicism genuine? During our imprisonment we have seen other Catholics, those of our adversaries. We have admired the religious conviction and devoutness of the British, the Australians, the Magyars and the Poles. Someone is likely to have observed the Americans and Canadians. Quite honestly, what impression does our religion make compared with theirs? If things have gone as they have during these last few years, perhaps it is because we have been insufficiently sincere Catholics.

It is also possible that there is another explanation for the absenteeism. Someone has realised that, essentially, he has been hoodwinked and betrayed; he does not know by whom or when, but he can see that his very being has been devastated. Confronted with this colossal disaster he finds himself overcome by a desire to blame someone, precisely who depends upon the individual; it ranges from God, the Pope, the King, il Duce, right down to the Italian people, the immigrants, the living, the dead, until, without reaching too far down the line someone will stop at the undersigned.

I do not wish to indulge in recriminations here; I just wish to ascertain what the facts might be. It is possible that hearing the truth is unpleasant, in this way . . .

The article continues on another page, which was not provided. The writer's name is at the end, so this is also missing. It is, indeed, a very sad piece.

The men in Camp 34 remained in Orkney until the spring of 1945, when they were moved to camps in Lancashire (no Italians remained in Orkney). This may explain why most articles say the Italians left Camp 60 at this time, as writers may have simply assumed they all left together. There were even more farewells and sorrowful partings as the Italians in Burray had had more opportunity to become known to local families.

A few left the small amounts of British money they had saved with friends in Orkney, because they feared it might be taken from them during the strict searches that still took place when changing camps. Months later, when Italians wrote to say they had reached home, the money was duly posted as agreed. Gino Caprara recalls:

*

Many of us used to make rings from half crowns, or make cigarette lighters and other items. Some of these were given as presents to our civilian friends but some were sold. I was in possession of a small amount of savings (about three pounds) when we were about to be transferred. We knew that every time we moved from one camp to another we had to be subjected to a severe search. The purpose of searching us was (I think) to avoid us being in possession of knives or arms of any kind. This had happened each time we had moved between camps, starting in Egypt.

Now, you may not like to know that not all the British soldiers in charge with that task behaved correctly. Some (a very few) availing themselves of the precarious situation, got possession of our money, watches, cigarettes or even wallets containing photographs. (Now I want to point out that I have no grudge against anyone. There was a war on and good and bad people might be met in all countries.)

Mindful of the past searches, the evening I paid my last visit to say goodbye to my friends, I left my modest savings with them and they promised to post this to me when things had returned to normal. I am glad to say that they maintained their promise and we kept in touch for years. When I returned to Orkney in 1992, very sadly I came to know that both had died.

The Italians' journey to their next camp was not without its more serious moments and in one transitional camp they came up against an attitude that was alien to them during their time in Orkney. Gino explains:

The camp was a disused cotton mill. As soon as we arrived the British Commandant assembled us in the square and with his stick under his arm got up on to the platform and spoke to us by saying, 'I hate you. In front of my office there is a board. Read it! All those who do not strictly follow these orders will be punished. That is all!'

We had no beds, only a straw mattress on the floor. In the morning we had to leave the mattresses and the blankets folded, arranged perfectly and go out. All day we had to hang around the camp because it was forbidden to enter the dormitory and we were anxious not to make infractions to the orders written on the board. The British sentries were old men and were friendly with us but they did their best not to show it. I think they had received severe orders by the official. Luckily, as it was only a transit camp we left after a few days.

I was one of those who went to Lancashire and stayed in a camp on the outskirts of Bury (Heywood). We formed a unit of Italian Labour Battalion and were employed in MU35 (maintenance unit 35) under the control of the Royal Air Force.

I remained there until my repatriation, which took place in April 1946. I returned to normal life at home on 20th May, having been away for six years and four months.

Domenico was based in Kew for his last ten months in Britain and was part of a gang transported each day to help repair or clear buildings. To see more of London they bribed the driver with cigarettes and chocolate to take different routes. He finally left for home, sailing from Southampton to Naples. He met up with his parents, brothers and sisters again in February 1946, six years and eight months since he had last seen them.

On the same ship was Ugo Pizzi, clutching the cloth case he had found on the Lamb Holm beach. His home was in the small village where he had been born, Fontanelle, which is in the province of Parma. Ugo sent a telegram to inform his wife and family that he was back in Italy and would return home the following day. His son Alberto picks up the story:

In the evening of the following day he arrived by train in Parma, boarded a bus going to the nearest village then started walking home. Two kilometres from his village he stopped at his uncle's home and his niece ran to Fontanelle to tell us. The news of his return immediately spread amongst our neighbours who came out and started running with me and my mum to meet him.

We had to follow the bank of a river but there was such a strong wind that we all had to go down to the meadows underneath. I remember him wearing a long grey-green coat and I can still feel the wind on my skin. The following morning my mother said he got up, cleaned his old bike and went looking for a job.

He seldom talked about his time in Orkney and none of the men from Camp 60 came from this part of Italy, so he had no contact with other ex-POWs after the war. We are convinced that the daily sufferings of being so far from home for years, with no news from his family, whose precarious life he was perfectly aware of, induced him to remove a large part of that experience from his memory.

We never wanted to force him to remember because we knew those years when he was forced to spend time away from his family still hurt him, but when he passed away in 1974 (from a disease linked to the malaria he caught during the war) we realised we knew too little about him and were sorry for not asking him to tell us more.

My father was a humble bricklayer, but thanks to his many sacrifices he managed to give us a better life. Both my brother and I could study, graduate and practise a profession. He was a proper man.

During the summer of 1994 Alberto's daughter Felicia was living in Edinburgh while taking an English course. She remembered hearing about Orkney as a child and over a free weekend made her way via John O'Groat's and the ferry to Kirkwall where, for the first time, she learnt about the chapel on Lamb Holm.

Two years later, Alberto and his wife Angela made their first journey to Orkney in order to start putting together the pieces of Ugo's life in Camp 60. On another visit, Alberto's brother Angelo found an old black and white photograph in the library archives of a group of men standing around a concrete bowling alley . . . a group of men that included his father Ugo.

'Much later, I spent quite some time searching for the family of Domenico Chiocchetti and finally traced Fabio, Angela and Letizia,' said Alberto. 'We met in Moena and are now firm friends.'

But there was one more question for Alberto. So many men, of all nationalities, went to war when their sons and daughters were small and returned, years later,

Concrete bowling alley, complete with concrete balls. The man picked out in the image is Ugo Pizzi. In 2003, his son Angelo discovered the image of his father while visiting Orkney. *Source: Orkney Library Archives. Photograph by James W. Sinclair.*

when those children were by then perhaps eight or nine, but with no memory of their father. Angelo was born after his father's return but Alberto was five when Ugo was repatriated.

While the memory of my father's return is still alive, the following months have almost faded away, maybe because my mum and relatives had told me about him so many times that I felt I already knew him.

Looking at his picture, my mother said I had once asked, 'Is my father really a big man?'

The truth is, thanks to his nature, my father was from the start, a sweet and serene presence in my life, even if I remember well his worries and anguish for the lack of work in the years following the end of the war.

The last flash of memory I have dates back to the autumn of 1945, just a few months before his return. A neighbour gave us something rare at that time, an exotic fruit we had never seen before, but it was still unripe.

Waiting for it to ripen, my mum put it on the mantelpiece and we decided together we would eat it with my father. The fruit ripened long before his return and sadly we had to eat it without him. I was so sorry. I still remember it as if it was yesterday.

Roberto Pendini arrived in Naples in June 1946 and spent eight days trying to reach his home in Vicenza.

'Italy was totally destroyed,' said Roberto. 'I was not married then but was reunited with my family and lucky enough to find a job after a month with a textile company.'

While he was at the Skipton camp Sergeant Major Guerrino Fornasier fell in love with a local girl whose parents were Italian. He was repatriated but Leda managed to travel to Italy and they were married in Florence. They came back to Britain and he worked in his wife's parents' ice cream business, which they expanded, moving the factory to Keighley in West Yorkshire. His daughter Gina takes up the story:

The first time I knew that my father had been in Orkney was when a neighbour was telling him he had just come back from there, where he had been deep-sea diving. The neighbour had come across a chapel that the Italian prisoners had made (not knowing my father had been one of them). He got a shock when my father turned around and coolly said, 'Yes, I know, I helped to build it.' Being young, I didn't know how significant it was, so never spoke about it much after that.

A few ex-POWs did not return to Italy at all. Guido DeBonis, who had been a farmer before the war, was one of them.

'One day during 1944 Major Buckland asked the men in Camp 60 if anyone wanted to move south to work on farms in England,' said Guido. 'I thought it would be warmer and was the first person to arrive at a camp in Ledbury. I was taken to a farm in Bushley, near Tewkesbury, and worked with another Italian called Giuseppe Dallo.'

Guido became friendly with the farmer, Mr Spry, and his family. Sixty-five years later, on 30th March 2009, the farmer's daughter attended Guido's ninetieth birthday celebrations.

One day, while I was busy haymaking, a girl came cycling along the road. I didn't want to go back to Italy then . . . she later became my wife! But any prisoners wishing to stay had to obtain permission from Mr Churchill. We had to report to the local police station for well over two years after the war ended, and if we got into any trouble we were warned that we would be deported.

Guido and Joyce married in secret and moved to a milk and fruit farm in Evesham where a cottage went with the job. However, not everyone in the nearby village was pleased with the situation and they faced some hostility for a while. Some of Joyce's family were not pleased either and for many years certain members would not have Guido in their home.

'I understood their feelings. We had been the enemy and while British soldiers were fighting and risking their lives, we were living in safety and being fed well.'

Guido later moved back near Bushley and, for a short period, was employed once again by Mr Spry, before taking a job at a nearby farm where he stayed until his retirement. He and Joyce had two sons and a daughter.

Over the years, the guides in Orkney hear stories from tourists that relate to the chapel's history and the following, from Fran Flett Hollinrake, is particularly moving.

I sometimes take coach parties to the chapel and one day there was a group of folk from England. One old lady on the tour told me this story. She was born and brought up in Lincolnshire, married and had children early on. She was widowed quite young, and once the children left home she started taking part in local activities.

This lady met a man (Italian) who lived on a nearby farm, and he told her he had been imprisoned in Orkney during the war. In 1944, he had left the camp and travelled to England where he had become a road engineer, saving enough money to buy a small farm. He never went back to Italy, and never had a family of his own.

These two elderly folk had quickly become great friends, and this developed into romance. The man related to her how he had been one of the Italians who had created the chapel in Orkney and how he had often wondered what it looked like now. The pair of them had checked in books and seen the chapel on TV, and they made a plan that one day they would travel to Orkney together so he could show her the place that had meant so much to him. They had booked the trip. Sadly, six months before they were due to leave, he passed away without ever seeing the chapel again.

The lady herself was telling me this story inside the chapel. She had decided to make the trip. As she stood in the chapel she said to me, 'I can feel him here. He's all around me.' She then showed me his photo in the line up of all those who contributed — and he was so handsome! The old lady said that he was very good looking in later life, too! By the time she had finished telling me this story, everybody else was back on the coach and the pair of us were having a good old weep.

I have never forgotten the tale. I was so lucky to meet her, and felt very privileged that she shared her private moment with me.

Despite subsequent publicity in Lincolnshire newspapers this lady could not be traced, so the identity of the craftsman who worked on the chapel and spent the remainder of his life as a farmer in England remains a mystery.

Exactly how many Italians were held in captivity during the construction of the Churchill Barriers has been an impossible figure to confirm. Most articles say that 1,200 arrived in Orkney at the beginning of 1942. However, the majority of articles also say there were around 500–550 in each camp, which leaves a few men unaccounted for.

W. S. Hewison's phenomenal work, *This Great Harbour Scapa Flow*, says that the figure peaked at 1,200 during 1943, but that the normal total was 970. Gino Caprara says the split was 500 men in Camp 60 and 553 in Camp 34.

The only documentary evidence discovered is the report on Camp 60 by Colonel Lynch, the Inspector of POW camps, which states that, in September

1942, there were 403 Italians on Lamb Holm. It would certainly appear that the numbers were not static, which probably accounts for the differing figures. While Italians continued to arrive in Orkney, men discovered to have particular skills were sometimes sent to other camps in Britain where their talents could be put to better use.

Ex-POWs, like Guido DeBonis, had to adhere to strict guidelines, set by the British Government, if they wanted to live in Great Britain after the war.

Aliens Order 1920. Certificate of Registration
NOTICE TO THE HOLDER OF THIS CERTIFICATE.

1. Before you effect a *permanent* change of residence (from the last address shown in this Certificate) you must give the Police of the district in which you reside your new address and the date on which you intend to move.

2. If your new residence is in another Police District you must, within 48 hours of your arrival there, report to the Police of the new district.

3. A *temporary* absence of less than 14 days from your permanent

residence need not be reported, but if such absence exceeds 14 days you must report your temporary address and all subsequent changes of address (*including* your return home) to the Police of the district where you are registered. *This may be done by letter.*

4. If you stay at an hotel, lodging-house, boarding-house or other place where lodging is provided for payment, you must, *on arrival*, write your name, nationality, the number of this Certificate, and the address from which you have come, and, *before leaving*, must write the address to which you intend to go on the form provided for the purpose.

5. You must report to the Police of the district where you are registered, within 48 hours, any change in any of the personal particulars given within (including professional or occupational) also marriage, divorce, or death of husband or wife.

6. Your children, if not British, must have separate Certificates when they reach the age of 16.

Failure to comply with any of the above requirements, making any false statement with regard to registration or with regard to this certificate, altering this certificate or any entry upon it, refusing to produce this certificate when legally required to do so or having in possession or using without lawful authority any forged, altered or irregular certificate, passport or other document concerned with registration, will render the offender liable to be detained in custody and to a fine of £100 or six months' imprisonment.

15
The Bleak Years

On 12th May 1945, a few days after VE Day, the Churchill Barriers were officially opened by the First Lord of the Admiralty, the Rt Hon. A. V. Alexander. Strict wartime censorship and regulations on travel resulted in a large number of the people living in Orkney's northern islands being unaware that the barriers had been built at all.

Even by the time they were opened officially, some were surprised to hear of their existence. The event was rather hastily arranged, which caught out a few local dignitaries. Patrick Sutherland Graeme attended the ceremony along with admiralty personnel and Gordon Nicol.

While leading figures celebrated a great feat of engineering and people marvelled at the ease with which they could travel, the little chapel remained locked in its cage, perhaps not quite forgotten but unable to be cared for. The camp looked derelict. Weeds had broken up the concrete paths that the Italians had laid so carefully and the previously well-tended borders were in ruin. The dragon looked up with scorn at St George, with his growing white hat, deposited by the gulls who found it a good resting place.

The speed with which the barriers were constructed, with some rubble not compacted and the sides built much more steeply than usual, would present the Orkney Islands Council with some major headaches in later years. Indeed, within two years of their completion the causeways had settled in some areas by more than two feet, which required significant reconstruction work. However, this should not detract from the enormous achievement of the barriers' creation.

The official opening of the Churchill Barriers took place on 12th May 1945, a few days after VE Day. Here, Patrick Sutherland Graeme and Admiral Macnamara are being shown a brochure that was produced for the occasion. *Source: Orkney Library Archives.*

In the immediate post-war years the evidence of war around the islands was gradually removed. Orkney, like the rest of Britain, was trying to get back to normality. The huge cableways were dismantled and taken elsewhere (one being used years later to build the Sloy Dam, part of the Sloy Hydro Scheme near Loch Lomond). The diggers and cranes were transported to England where they were in great demand. The trains that had travelled backward and forward so many times were taken away to transport other goods on different journeys.

The remains of fortifications from both world wars can be seen even to this day, such as concrete observation posts and gun emplacements. They were

Barrier number one, connecting mainland Orkney (right) with Lamb Holm. To the left of the barrier, on Lamb Holm, is the block-making yard and beyond that, Camp 60. Barriers two and three, connecting Glimps Holm to Lamb Holm and Burray are also visible, along with several of the blockships. *Source: Orkney Library Archives.*

probably considered to require too much effort and cost to remove. However, the POW camps were meant to be demolished and the land returned to the state it was in before the war, as far as was feasible to do so.

This meant that Camp 60 and Camp 34 were also to be taken apart and Balfour Beatty was given the contract. Fate had other ideas in mind. One of the gang of Balfour Beatty men given the job of dismantling the Lamb Holm camp was joiner Thomas Alexander Thomson, who lived all his life in St Margaret's Hope on South Ronaldsay. His daughter Margaret (who used to watch the booms open and close with her grandmother) now lives in Dumbarton, just outside Glasgow, and she takes up his story:

My father had quite a bit of contact with the Italians in Lamb Holm and saw the chapel as it was being built. He was a painter as well as a joiner and appreciated the skill of the images that had been created inside the chapel. He spoke about it often to my mother. After the war, when he was one of the Balfour Beatty workers given the task of dismantling Camp 60, he was very upset at the idea of touching the chapel.

He was a very quiet man and an elder in the Church of Scotland. Father felt that such a holy place should be left alone. 'We canna tak it doon,' he had said to my mother at the time. Father spoke to the other men and they obviously felt the same way. In the end, when the camp was gone, the little chapel and statue remained.

So the chapel and the statue were left alone, the only reminders of Camp 60, apart from the concrete bases of the Nissen huts. People tried to put the war behind them and started taking holidays. Orkney was a popular destination and the chapel's fame spread as an increasing number of people gazed upon Domenico's image of the Madonna and Child. Local people also liked to visit the gem on their doorstep.

However, no one looked after the building. The winter winds and rain beat it without mercy until cracks appeared in the roof and water began to seep in, staining the paintings and damaging the plasterboard. Giuseppe's beautiful rood screen began to rust, while the tiny cross on top of the bell tower had deteriorated so badly that part of it had snapped off.

The chapel was left alone in the camp when the men were moved to Yorkshire in September 1944. *Source: Orkney Library Archives. Photograph by James W. Sinclair.*

The main, west-facing door had rotted badly and no longer provided much protection against the weather, or mice. Even more worrying was that a gap had opened up between the façade and the hut. Pennisi's stunning bas-relief of the face of Christ had been pounded until the fine detail had started to wear away. And although the bell rang out its warning across the empty island, like a ship in distress, there was no one to hear it except the gulls or the guillemots, known locally as 'tysties'.

Nor did every visitor appreciate just what they were standing in, and one day someone wrote their name on the wall. It's a strange trait of human nature that nobody had done such a thing before, but once they had, others followed like sheep and soon much of the walls were defaced. By 1958, the building was in a pitiful state and it was its deteriorating condition that galvanised local people into action.

The driving force was Father Joseph-Ryland Whitaker, the Catholic priest for Orkney and Shetland from 1953 to 1961. He spent most of his time in Lerwick but the plight of the little chapel was brought to his attention during one of his visits. He helped to form a group of local people into the Italian Chapel Preservation Committee, which still plays an active and vital role today in maintaining the building for future generations.

The first meeting of the committee was held in June 1958. Father Whitaker took on the role of chairman, Patrick Sutherland Graeme (who was by then Lord Lieutenant of Orkney) was president and his daughter Alison the secretary. The treasurer was Cecil Walls and Ernest Marwick was press secretary. The latter was the same man who had been manager of J. M. Stevenson when the lovesick Italian had handed over his letter to the shop assistant in 1944. By 1958, Ernest Marwick had put his shopkeeping days far behind him and was working for the *Orkney Herald*.

Patrick Sutherland Graeme had more than once expressed alarm at the condition of the chapel, but he had been told by various people that the materials it was constructed of made the building impossible to preserve. However, the situation had reached a stage where either something had to be done, or the building would be lost for ever. The problem facing the committee was what to do.

Virtually nothing appeared to have been published about Father Whitaker and Father Cairns, who had later become involved in the early days of saving the chapel, and there were no leads to follow. A letter sent to the Bishop of Aberdeen, whose diocese includes Orkney, received a response to say that there was no information other than that both men had been Jesuit priests. Ged Clapson, communications officer for the Society of Jesus: British Province was, therefore, contacted.

'The thing about Jesuit priests is that they always keep a good record of their lives,' said Ged. He was certainly right with this observation and soon sent details of the relevant parts of each priest's 'mini autobiography'.

In his account about the period he spent as a Catholic priest in Orkney and Shetland, Father Whitaker gives a very interesting slant on why the chapel had fallen into such disrepair between the time the Italians left the islands and the formation of the chapel preservation committee, approximately fifteen years later.

On 24th April, 1958, I left Shetland on board the *St Ninian* to take over the church in Orkney. Father Robert McDonald had left on 21st April to go to Dornie. During his two years at Orkney he had redecorated the church very beautifully, and had won the esteem and affection, not only of the Catholics, but of many of the non-Catholics as well.

When he moved out, of course, he took all his possessions with him, but a Jesuit moving in can bring very little, and hence there were some serious gaps in the furnishings: no blankets, sheets nor pillowcases, no kettle, teapot nor frying pan, no house-keeper, and only £30 in the bank. I had an old sleeping bag, a relic from the First World War — that served for bedding and tea could be made in a pan.

But very soon the parishioners rallied round: one brought a pair of sheets, another a blanket, and others brought things for the kitchen. When the bishop heard of my plight he sent £100, and thus the immediate problems were solved.

There are about thirty Catholics in Kirkwall who attend mass regularly. Many others are scattered over the islands and can only hear mass when the priest visits them. A Catholic doctor, with his wife and family, live on the island of Sanday. The priest visits them once a month by boat to say mass and catechise the children. He has to stay overnight and return home by boat the next day. It is a great event for the family and the children all get a holiday from school.

The next task was to find out if anything could be done to preserve the chapel on the island of Lamb Holm, some eight miles from Kirkwall, which had been constructed by the Italian prisoners of war, interned there in 1943 [sic] and 1944. It is a wonderful little chapel because it was constructed out of scrap material of all sorts. It has become one of the sights of Orkney. Yet it was rapidly falling into disrepair and nothing was being done to save it. Why was this?

The priest in Orkney had always presumed that the Lord Lieutenant of the County, who owned the chapel, was not anxious to preserve it, since in fact little had been done to conserve it. The Lord Lieutenant on the other hand was wondering why the Catholic authorities did not interest themselves in this lovely little shrine. And thus the matter stood for fifteen years.

As soon as I phoned Mr Sutherland Graeme, the Lord Lieutenant, the deadlock was solved. He was delighted that something would now be done, gave me permission to form a small committee for the preservation of the chapel and agreed to act as its president. Unfortunately, he died soon after the committee had been formed at a meeting in Kirkwall on 22nd June, but his daughter agreed to take his place. One of the first actions of the committee was to place a collecting-box in the chapel and during the summer last year visitors contributed over £100. This has been used to do repairs most urgently needed.

The committee already had some money at its disposal because visitors sometimes left donations in the holy water stoup.

'For years my aunt Alison collected the money left in the chapel, long before there was a safe, emptying it into a dustsheet and carrying it home,' said Sheena Wenham. 'I remember us all on the floor of her sitting room counting away.'

The most urgent repairs needed were to stop any more water getting into the building and to make the façade safe. It was agreed that the relevant local tradesmen would be contacted to start this work as soon as possible.

Longer term, the chapel needed extensive repairs to the structure of the building and significant restoration work to the interior. There was no doubt that the best person to carry out the painting was Domenico Chiocchetti, but no one had heard from him since he had left the islands in 1944. Nobody had any idea of his address nor, indeed, knew if he was still alive.

The committee needed outside help and decided to contact the BBC to see if they would be interested in the plight of the little chapel and whether they could help find an Italian who had been a POW in Orkney during the Second World War. Domenico's daughter Letizia explained how her father was tracked down.

The BBC broadcast a programme about the chapel and asked if anyone had details of the ex POWs who were involved in its creation. Mr and Mrs Harvey in Skipton were the only people in Britain with my father's address and they happened to hear the programme. They contacted the BBC, which telephoned the town hall in Moena explaining that they were trying to get in touch with the artist who had painted the Madonna and Child in the chapel in Orkney.

Of course, in those days, no one in a small village had a telephone in their home. A message was sent to my father to arrive at the town hall at a certain time so that he could take a telephone call from the BBC in England! He was very surprised and had not realised there was such interest in it that people would go to so much trouble to speak to him.

Charles Ricono was the BBC's South European Productions Supervisor and he later interviewed Domenico by telephone. Programmes were subsequently broadcast on the BBC's Home Service and Italian radio. Further programmes were planned once restoration work on the chapel began.

Interest in the chapel continued to spread. The BBC's religious broadcasting department offered to pay Domenico's expenses to travel to Orkney and stay there for three weeks while he carried out restoration work on the paintings. A great number of preparations had to be put in place to make the trip

Domenico Chiocchetti, March 1960. *Source: Orkney Library Archives.*
Photograph by James W. Sinclair.

feasible and a proposed date was set for the following year. Domenico had
wanted his friend Pennisi to also be invited but this did not happen. The artist
wrote a letter to Charles Ricono and this was translated and sent to Ernest
Marwick.*

I learn with pleasure that the committee will concern itself with the manual
work involved in restoring the chapel. This means a saving of time for me

* OA Ref D31/27/2

as I shall be able to concentrate on the decoration. As regards the paint, I expect I can obtain it in Kirkwall (it was obtainable there even during the war). They are in any case tempera colours made up as a paste and packed in glass jars. I do not know how the colours have stood up to the weather, nor to what extent they have faded, but I shall be able to check this when I am there.

As far as I am concerned it is difficult to say until I have seen the chapel how long the work of painting will take; I certainly shan't be able to stay more than a month. With regard to my knowledge of English it is not very good but I think I shall succeed in making myself understood. It was really extremely kind of the committee to express concern in case I should be unhappy amongst people who do not speak Italian.

I do not think they need worry. When one is the guest of people as kind as the inhabitants of the Orkneys, it is easy to make oneself understood in the universal language of art. Would you please thank Mr Marwick and all the inhabitants of Kirkwall on my behalf? I really feel honoured by so much kindness.

When I am once again alone in the chapel at Lamb Holm with my paints and brushes I know that I shall feel 'at home'. I promise to do all that lies in my power so that the restoration may be successful and meet with the approval of the committee and the inhabitants. Meanwhile I thank you all most warmly.

The retired Lt Colonel Buckland was also contacted during 1959, at his home in Shropshire. His reply to Ernest Marwick includes a comment on how the building of the chapel helped the well-being of the Italians.

Some critics might say that to create such a work of art to subsequently become a museum piece was a waste of time and materials — but as the poet says, a thing of beauty is a joy for ever. The chapel was a tremendous help in building up the morale of the prisoners and the effect could be seen in the building of the Churchill Barriers.

16
Domenico Returns

Work was extremely scarce in Italy after the end of the Second World War as much of the country's infrastructure had been decimated. Back in Moena, Domenico set up a small business as a house painter, employing a handful of men. As he once commented: 'In a little village one can't survive only with art!' When Domenico was contacted by the chapel preservation committee he wrote to them:*

Dear Friends in Orkney,

I have great pleasure in replying to the invitation of your newspaper to tell my story of the chapel of the Italian prisoners of war in the island of Lamb Holm. The fact is that after all that Father Giacobazzi has so well and so comprehensively written, there is not much I can add. But one thing I feel I ought to do, or rather, must do, is to express to you all, my friends, my very real pleasure and warm thanks for the interest with which, after such a long interval of time, you regard our chapel and for the fine sentiment which has induced you to form a committee, whose aims will be to see to the repairs and the maintenance of the characteristic structure of the shrine, thereby making of it a symbol and a remembrance.

I have been touched by your initiative and, let me admit it, have been filled with legitimate pride. I must say too that the time spent in prison has been for

* OA Ref 31/27/4

me transmitted into something precious if it has allowed me, along with my dear companions, to create a work which you have shown that you hold in such high esteem.

During these recent times I have, with feelings of great emotion, been going over in my mind again the day on which, while talking with Father Giacobazzi, there came to me the idea of the chapel — the meeting with the fine commandant of the camp Colonel Buckland and his 'Bravo' of encouragement when I said that it was my desire to make the chapel a work of beauty and dignity. And it was so!

I remember the enthusiasm for the work of my companions to whom I assigned particular sectors in which to operate. My own special activities were devoted, above all, to modelling in clay the parts of the altar and the various figures with which I then adorned it; little columns, a stoup for the holy water, angels and evangelists. But most of all I remember my own dear Madonna of the Olive (the Madonna of the Peace) which, while war was raging over all the world, came from my brush like an invocation the more ardently evoked because of exile and the privations from which I was suffering.

All the same, it was not without a sense of sadness, that at the end of the war, I left the island of Lamb Holm because that little church and that Madonna depicted above the altar had remained in my heart and I felt I was leaving a part of myself.

With what joy I shall see again after so many years the little church and with what renewed enthusiasm I shall attend to the repairs, which the usage of time has rendered necessary and the perfecting of the work which the changed conditions and the possibility of procuring material to work with (not just the makeshift material provided by chance) will permit me.

Again, my heartfelt thanks, Orcadian friends, and liveliest congratulations for the activities of your committee united to my earnest hopes and prayers that your chapel and mine may remain always to inspire in all who visit it thoughts of peace and brotherhood.

One cold morning in March 1960, Ernest Marwick and Father Cairns stood waiting at Kirkwall airport. Father Frank Cairns had moved to Orkney in 1958 and taken over the role of chairman from Father Whitaker, who remained in Lerwick as the Catholic priest for Shetland. They were expecting two men on the plane that was due to arrive from Inverness. One man was Charles Ricono.

Chiocchetti is greeted at Kirkwall airport in 1960 by Father Cairns (left) and Ernest Marwick. *Source: Orkney Library Archives. Photograph by James W. Sinclair.*

The other had last arrived in Orkney as a POW. Now, Domenico Chiocchetti was an honoured guest. It must have been extraordinary for the artist to see the chapel without any other part of Camp 60 remaining. There were no huts, no barbed-wire fence or concrete punishment block. The drive to Lamb Holm must have been surreal, with all the mess of construction and war removed. Even the huge Blondins no longer dominated the skyline.

One can only wonder at the conflicting emotions felt by Domenico when he entered the chapel for the first time in sixteen years. Although he had been in contact with the preservation committee during the previous year, so had some idea of the condition of the building, he must have been desperate to see how much it had actually deteriorated. In an interview at the time he said: 'It is no use trying to describe what I felt; no journalist could write it. I was moved to tears.'

He had only three weeks to help restore the building. Fortunately, a small team of local people were ready to lend a hand, including a Kirkwall man called Stanley Hall who had carried out, under the guidance of the preservation committee, a significant amount of preparation work during the weeks leading up to Domenico's arrival. His son Robert, who today runs a barber's shop in Kirkwall, explained how his father became involved:

My father had been in the Royal Navy and was based for a while in Scapa Flow, which was when he met my mother who was a teacher in Orkney. He went on many patrols and I still have his five campaign medals. During the North African landings he was badly injured and ended up being taken, along with the damaged ship, all the way to America where he spent a year in hospital. He was released the same day that the repaired ship came out of dry dock, although I think that was a coincidence!

After the war, my parents came back to Orkney where my mother picked up her teaching career, my father never again being in good health. However, the newly formed chapel preservation committee hired him to carry out a series of basic repairs before Domenico arrived. This included jobs such as sanding down and repainting the badly rusted rood screen and replacing parts of the plasterboard that had been too damaged by water to save.

This meant that the surface of the walls were ready to paint. Although my father wasn't an artist he worked closely with Domenico during his three weeks in Orkney and the two men became good friends. He helped again when Domenico returned in 1964. The two men kept in touch until my father's death in 1981. In a way it was ironic, because my father had been a seaman on one of the ships that brought the Italian POWs from Aberdeen to Orkney at the beginning of 1942. The chapel helped to make friends of former enemies.

Domenico's task was mainly one of painting but a significant amount of work was carried out during his three-week stay in Orkney. A variety of tradesmen called to help to ensure that, as his visit came to an end, all repairs to windows and doors had been carried out.

On 10th April 1960, the day before Domenico was to leave Orkney, a service of rededication was held and some of this was subsequently broadcast on Italian radio. The event was attended by more than 200 Orcadians, who represented a wide cross-section of denominations. Domenico was the first person to receive Holy Communion. During the service, Father Whitaker said:

Chiocchetti retouching the Madonna and Child during his return visit to Orkney in 1960. *Source: Orkney Library Archives. Photograph by James W. Sinclair.*

Of the buildings clustering on Lamb Holm in wartime only two remain: this chapel and the statue of St George. All the things which catered for material needs have disappeared, but the two things which catered for spiritual needs still stand. In the heart of human beings the truest and most lasting hunger is for God.

During his three weeks working on the chapel Domenico prepared a letter to the people of Orkney and he presented this to the preservation committee on his departure. The letter is in the Orkney library archives but is not in his handwriting, so was probably written at the time by someone with a better grasp of English.*

Dear Orcadians,

My work at the chapel is finished. In these three weeks I have done my best to give again to the little church that freshness which it had sixteen years ago. The chapel is yours — for you to love and preserve. I take with me to Italy the remembrance of your kindness and wonderful hospitality. I shall remember always, and my children shall learn from me to love you.

* OA Ref D31/27

[177]

I thank the authorities of Kirkwall, the courteous preservation committee and all those who directly or indirectly have collaborated for the success of this work and for having given me the joy of seeing again the little chapel of Lamb Holm where I, in leaving, leave a part of my heart. Thanks also in the name of all my companions of Camp 60 who worked with me. Goodbye dear friends of Orkney — or perhaps I should say just 'au revoir.'

Domenico Chiocchetti

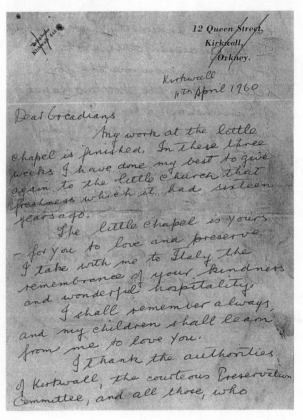

Chiocchetti's famous letter, which he left behind for the people of Orkney after his three-week stay in 1960 to repair the chapel.
Source: *Orkney Library Archives.*

When Domenico knew he was returning to Britain he asked the preservation committee for the address of Thomas Buckland and later wrote to him. The retired officer's doctor would not let him make the journey to Orkney for Domenico's visit, so once he had completed his work on the chapel the artist travelled to Shropshire and spent a few days with his old friend.

Soon after Domenico returned to Moena, a group of local artists formed a workshop to produce sacred woodcarvings. He gave up his decorating business and joined them as a decorator of statues, spending all his spare time painting. This included a significant number of floral designs on farmhouse-style furniture, made by a local company. He also took part in many art exhibitions, art having been a passion throughout his life.

His visit to Orkney generated publicity both inside and outside the UK. In his home in Savona, Celso Santini saw an article about Domenico in a magazine. He used to play guitar in the Camp 60 band but had lost touch with the artist after repatriation. He wrote to Domenico.

Dear Chiocchetti,

I have asked myself on many occasions how our friends and fellow prisoners from Camp 60 had ended up. The task of tracing someone is indeed arduous, basically because many things changed after the war and it is common to forget everything that refers to prison life, even if we do not manage to eliminate some of its episodes from our memories.

I have, on many occasions, remembered at least those with whom I had a particularly close friendship due, perhaps, to sharing a specific activity in the camp. For example, the memory of you remains alive because I acted in the northerners' theatre group (La Compagnia Settentrionale). Do you remember? There was also a theatre group formed by the southerners (Terrun).

You were in overall charge of our group, Sforza, the chap from Terni, was the principal comic, and yours truly was the modest principal actor. If I think about it, I start to laugh, yet we spent a great number of happy and carefree hours on that stage!

I would enter on stage with a guitar, rest one foot on the stool, and launch into (Paolo) Tosti's song 'Ideale'. I am certain that if even only one of Tosti's distant relatives had heard me, I would have been shot; and yet, this was enough, even if only for a short spell, for us to forget our troubles.

Then you threw yourself, body and soul, into the building of the Chapel to the extent that you abandoned us; but, perhaps more than we did, you managed to escape from the sadness of our lives. Now, after many long years, the old and dear chapel has provided you with a way to become known, and, from what I hear, half of Italy and half of Britain has spoken of, and continues to speak of, you.

Well done Chiocchetti! I am happy for you because you deserve it.

After the interlude of Skipton, we returned to our respective homes and we lost touch with each other — each following his own path, intent on having a family and recovering some of that lost time.

Since then I have neither seen nor heard from anyone, apart from the one occasion on which the Genoese lad Burlando, that incomparable mechanic who used to fix the vehicles used in the Lamb Holm project (remember?), appeared at my house. Then I lost touch with him. In 1948, I put to sea and, during my voyages, had occasion to land in Britain, but always in places which were too far from those which I knew.

Some time ago, while browsing through the weekly magazine Gente, *a photograph of you and your family caught my eye. Well, you won't believe this, but before reading the article which was about you and the Chapel, I remained transfixed for some minutes looking at the picture of you, because, even without knowing what it was about, I instantly recognised your face and, I can assure you, that, while several years have gone by, you have not changed a bit!*

As soon as I realised that it was really you, I read the whole article in the twinkling of an eye, and a highly emotional memory of those days engulfed me; and if I once did all I could to forget that period of my life, this time I wanted, as much as was possible, to remember every single day, starting from that first day when we disembarked onto that bare, raw island, still in the same condition as when God had created it, when not even the [Nissen] huts had been built (remember?)*. And the mud in the camp, which reached up to our knees, no lighting, and, what was worse, nothing to eat.

We did not lose heart, and began to fill the island with string nooses to capture wild rabbits, which, using the excuse that they were unwell, Doctor Gerbino Rocco confiscated and ate them himself! How angry that made me then!

At this point my wife saw me with the journal in my hand and, seeing the tears in my eyes, wanted to know why. And so, just as though I were watching a film, from that day on I began to tell her the full story. I went off to rummage around, and somewhere found those few photographs we had, among which is the one of the orchestra, in which we both appear (in case you don't remember, I am the one with the guitar and the word POLA written on the sweater).

* Santini's comment that Camp 60 had not been built when the Italians arrived on Lamb Holm contradicts other accounts.

As you see, my dear Chiocchetti, the world is indeed small. Having seen you in the photograph with your wonderful family, believe me, I cannot but congratulate you sincerely. I am happy that all is heading in the right direction for you, because you deserve it. I knew you when you were a thoroughly decent and very likeable lad.

I have been married for eleven years, but have no children. As far as work is concerned, I cannot complain; I am employed in a bank. For now I do not want to take up any more of your time, but believe me, these last ten minutes of recalling distant memories have really done me a power of good.

Should you want to write to me I would be very glad to hear from you. I hope that your fame will still permit you to set aside a few minutes for me. I am also sufficiently confident in the extent of the fame that, when I send this letter, even not knowing your exact address, I shall address it with just your name and the name of your village, with the certainty that you will receive it.

Domenico's trip to Orkney in 1960 was the catalyst for many visits between Orkney and Moena.

Maria and Domenico Chiocchetti during their visit to Orkney in 1964. *Source: Orkney Library Archives. Photograph by James W. Sinclair.*

'The following year Alison travelled to Moena,' said Sheena. 'Domenico presented her with a carved angel and she has valued greatly her friendship with the Chiocchetti family ever since.'

In 1964, Domenico returned to Orkney with his wife Maria, who was at last able to see the chapel that her husband had been so instrumental in creating. Their visit attracted wide coverage in both newspapers and on radio and for the duration of their stay they were Orkney's most famous guests.

As a gift, they brought with them the fourteen Stations of the Cross, depicting the Passion of Christ, which can be seen on the walls of the chapel to this day. They were carved in Moena and each is 8 x 6.5 inches in size. Maria also brought an altar cloth that she had made and this is still laid out on special occasions. In a letter to Ernest Marwick in 1966 she wrote:*

We remember very often our friends in Orkney, and always wish for news. Miss Linton writes us from time to time, giving us news of the chapel and of you all on the committee. The distance which separates us does not make us forget our friendship. On the contrary, it seems to me always to reinforce it the more.

Many months have already passed since our visit to Kirkwall, and it seems to me that I remember everything in detail. My children, especially Fabio, are always most interested in the history of the chapel, which he loves more and more, and of the people who preserve it.

During the late 1960s, an association was formed for the Italians who had been held in captivity in Orkney and this was quite active. Domenico was president.

In 1970, Domenico returned again, this time with his seventeen-year-old son Fabio and eldest daughter Letizia, who by this point was nineteen. Young Angela, at twelve, was happy to leave her trips to the chapel until later in life. It was a journey that all of them would make many times in the following years. Letizia remembers:

Of course, my father spoke often to my mother about the chapel, which he described in great detail. We were obviously too young but I remember

* OA Ref D31/27

Chiocchetti carrying out repairs to the façade in 1960. *Source: Orkney Library Archives. Photograph by James W. Sinclair.*

Dad telling us lots of stories, some of them entirely invented. Years later we realised the authenticity of one of them!

I had been dreaming of visiting Orkney for a long time, and excited to see the chapel. I remember examining every corner of it, plying my father with eager questions about how it was built and who was responsible for various parts of the work. We volunteered to help him repaint the front windows of the chapel, which simulates stained glass. The emotion on entering the chapel is still as great as that very first time.

By 1977, ill health forced Domenico to give up work and he spent his time painting small Christmas cards and watercolours. He was never again able to return to Orkney. Letizia again:

My father was always cheerful, certainly a good-natured and quiet person, a lover of nature and good music. He was helpful and unselfish. I remember

Chiocchetti studying his Madonna and Child during a return visit in 1970. *Source: Orkney Library Archives. Photograph by Dougie Shearer.*

Mum saying that often people delayed payments or didn't pay at all for his work as a house painter, so she had to collect the debt — he felt too embarrassed! We never heard him complaining about anything. He always tried to seek the positive side of life, even throughout the war.

Domenico's fame spread far beyond his home town of Moena in the Dolomites, where he was a well respected man. In 1996, at the age of eighty-six, he was granted the freedom of Moena.

In 1975, Sergeant Major 'Rino' Fornasier died of cancer at the age of fifty-nine. Stanley Boardman was the local sign writer in Keighley who used to create the signs for the ice cream vans belonging to the company Rino worked for. He was a good friend of the ex-Orkney POW. Following his death, Stanley Boardman wrote an article for *Yorkshire Life* magazine about his experience at the funeral.

It's nine o'clock on the morning of 24th October 1975. I am sitting, huddled against the cold, in a discreet corner of St Anne's Roman Catholic church in Keighley. In front of me, five or six seats. In front of these, resting on a chrome-plated wheeled trolley surrounded by tall, lighted candles, a plain oak coffin with a solitary wreath of flowers on its lid. Inside that coffin lies the body of one Guerrino Fornasier. I have known Rino, as we all affectionately knew him, for nigh on thirty years. He was without doubt, one of the finest men it has been my pleasure and privilege of meeting, working and associating with.

What I am going to tell you now must come somewhat of a shock to you, but it would not have shocked Rino because many was the time while working together we discussed this very point. Had I encountered Guerrino Fornasier a few years earlier, I would have shot him and I would have been shooting to kill. If I hadn't done this he would have shot me or thrust six inches of cold steel bayonet through my guts.

I wouldn't have wanted to shoot him. He wouldn't have wanted to shoot me. He wouldn't have wanted to twist that bayonet so that it did the ultimate damage before pulling it out of my body. But we would have had to. It would have been our duty, because I was T/125230 Driver Boardman

SR (RASC) of the British Army and he was Sergeant Guerrino Fornasier of the Italian Army.

Quite unknown to each other we were both in North Africa at the same time. Our superiors in their wisdom, or otherwise, had told us we were enemies, and trained us to kill. Fate decreed that he met up with some other British regiment, was taken prisoner, shipped to this country and put in a cage. Some years later the war came to an end and the cage door was opened.

Fate again stepped in and guided Guerrino Fornasier's feet to Keighley where he settled, married and had a beautiful daughter, built up a prosperous business and an ever-increasing circle of friends and admirers. Rino was loved by all who met him. Sitting all around me in this impressive

A picture of Sergeant Major Fornasier taken while he was in Camp 60. *Photograph by James W. Sinclair.*

looking building is a 50/50 ratio, black-haired, black-clothed Italians and pale, solemn-faced English people.

I am a man of no religion and feel slightly out of place sitting silently here, taking no part in the service, which I do not understand and is foreign to me. So my thoughts are of the friend I have lost and the agonizing sorrow of his heartbroken wife and daughter, and the grief of his hundreds of admirers who are going to miss him so much.

So, when Christmas comes this year I shall stop at some moment during the celebrations, and even though I have no religion, shall inwardly say a little prayer to someone, somewhere, in the hope that if there is anyone to receive it, he, or they will try to do something about putting sense into the heads of those who have hate and greed and violence in their hearts, so that never ever again would it be possible for anyone like Rino and I to be put in the terrible position where we would have had to try and kill each other.

As I stood outside the church and watched them load his coffin into the hearse I hoped that his Christian belief was right and my disbelief wrong, for, while it mattered not to either of us when he was alive, now that he was being taken on his last journey, I would be able to say with conviction something I have casually said to him a thousand times, 'Cheerio, Rino — see you later!'

17
The Priests

Shortly before the Italians left Camp 60 in September 1944 Padre Giacomo was suddenly taken ill and rushed to hospital (it is not clear whether he was in the Kirkwall Balfour hospital or the nearby military hospital). He was there for three months and it was during this period that his mother died. When he came out the men from Camp 60 had long gone to the camp in Yorkshire.

He spent some time at St Margaret's Hope on South Ronaldsay then was moved to a camp near Sheffield, before being repatriated. He landed at Naples on 16th June 1945 and travelled to his home town to see his brothers and sisters.

Italy was completely different from the country he had left in 1938. Apart from a brief period as a military chaplain, Padre Giacomo spent the remainder of his life in various Italian monasteries. He was involved in helping to extend a small chapel in Milano Marittima where he spent many years.

Padre Giacomo died in 1971 at the age of seventy-six and was buried in Missano, west of Bologna. In 1985, the nearby town of Pavullo nel Frignano honoured his memory by naming a street, *'Padre Giacomo Giacobazzi'*.

Occasionally in life, for good or bad, the actions of one person can have consequences that reverberate down the decades, affecting many who have no connection whatsoever with that person, their beliefs or culture.

Certainly, if in 1958, Father Joseph Ryland-Whitaker had not instigated the creation of a group of local Orkney people with the aim of preserving a derelict

The Camp 60 priest, Padre Giacomo, summer 1944. The image shows two power cables running from the nearest hut. *Photograph by James W. Sinclair.*

Nissen hut that stood alone on a tiny, windswept island, then today some 90,000 people a year would not enter its doors and gaze upon its wonders.

Fate is a funny old thing. Joe, as he was known as a young man, trained not for the priesthood, but to be a doctor. In 1915, at the age of nineteen, he started to study medicine, but the following year he was called up to join the Great War, just as Padre Giacomo had been in Italy during his studies to become a priest. Joe became a Second-Lieutenant in the Royal Field Artillery and was sent to France. Subsequently, he was awarded the MC for bravery in the field.

After the war, he continued with his studies and qualified as a LRCPS (Licentiate of the Royal College of Physicians and Surgeons) in Edinburgh in 1923, graduating three years later as a MBBS (Bachelor of Medicine and Bachelor of Surgery) in London. By 1928, he was living in Edinburgh, engaged

Father Whitaker was instrumental in saving the chapel from falling into ruin when he formed the chapel preservation committee in June 1958. He took the service of rededication in 1960 at the end of Chiocchetti's three-week visit to restore the chapel. *Source: Society of Jesus.*

in teaching medicine and in research work. However, his calling to the Catholic faith had reached a point where, in 1929, he began his novitiate at Roehampton. During his second year, he began to train some of the Brothers as infirmary workers.

He was ordained in 1936 and Brother Joseph became Father Whitaker. For the next seventeen years he held posts in Liverpool, Glasgow and London.

However, the Bishop of Aberdeen had asked the Society of Jesus for help in establishing a permanent mission in Shetland and, in 1953, Father Whitaker became the first priest in charge at Lerwick. Later, his work extended to include Orkney. This new field of apostolate was entirely after his own heart. In Shetland there were thirty-six Catholics, many of them lapsed, but no native Shetlanders among them. The church was not in use and in a state of disrepair. In his first account, Father Whitaker said:

'This is a real Jesuit apostolate, hard and hidden and humble, in the true tradition of our missionary history.'

His main work was 'frequent, friendly, preserving contact with the lapsed Catholics, and then the cultivation of friendly relations as far as possible with the non-Catholic population'. In 1961, Father Whitaker was transferred to Stornoway on the Isle of Lewis. He died suddenly in 1964 while working in Edinburgh. Upon his death, the *Orcadian* newspaper wrote:

> Although the longest continuous period that he spent in Orkney was six months, Fr Whitaker has been a regular visitor to the county since 1958, his most recent visit being only a few weeks before his death. He took the initiative in restoring the Italian Chapel. He found many willing helpers and the Italian Chapel Preservation Committee was established. He had the honour of celebrating mass and preaching to a congregation of 200 when the Chapel was eventually re-dedicated. He will be sadly missed by friends of many denominations in Orkney and Shetland.

In 1919, Frank Cairns was born in Camperdown Street, Glasgow, the youngest of ten children. These were grim years of unemployment and whilst most youngsters left school at fourteen, the older members of the family rallied to keep Frank at St Aloysius's College. On leaving school he joined the archdiocese and went for three years to the Scots College in Rome, where he gained a Bachelor of Philosophy, and then had a year's theology at St Peter's College, Bearsden.

He had, apparently, a great affection for his Jesuit teachers and years later, in 1941, he was released by the archdiocese and entered the novitiate at St Beuno's in North Wales. After one more year of philosophy, at Heythrop in Oxfordshire, he taught for four years at St Ignatius College, north London, before returning to Heythrop for theology and ordination. From 1953 to 1955 he was on the staff at Beaumont near Windsor and was succeeded there by Father Bamber, who later took over from him in Orkney. Father Bamber takes up the tale in the account of his own life.

It must have been in 1953 that Fr Cairns volunteered for the Northern Isles on the inspiration of Fr Whitaker, or was designated for this work. He glided into all that he did, or so it seemed. When he left the Scots

Father Cairns, the Catholic priest in Orkney between 1958 and 1963. During that time he was chairman of the chapel preservation committee. *Source: Society of Jesus.*

College in Rome for the Society, he was parted temporarily from friends whom he was to meet again in Scotland itself.

By that time he had gathered more friends in the Society and in the neighbourhood of Heythrop, putting to use on occasion his knowledge of Italian amongst Italian prisoners of war, and giving them such souvenirs or objects of piety as he knew would be welcome to them. This was a practice of his everywhere. He had just the knack of giving people what he knew would suit them.

In Shetland from 1955 to 1958 he played a modest second fiddle to Fr Whitaker, whose character and style he complemented in many respects, so that they presented a good team to Catholics and non-Catholics alike.

When the Society was asked to relieve the Aberdeen diocese of Orkney also, it was Fr Whitaker who went down to arrange the take-over, but both worked there for parts of the summer, assisted also by Fr Strachan. By November Fr Cairns was in charge. He always said, in his unselfish way, that Fr Whitaker had given him the choice of Orkney or Shetland, but his decision was probably prompted by what he thought Fr Whitaker would prefer, as the Provincial had left them to work it out between them.

Each Christmas in Shetland, Frank had organised a choir for what was really a showpiece service for the benefit of non-Catholics at midnight mass in Lerwick, and he did this for the last time during his first Christmas as parish priest in Orkney, before organising in subsequent years a similar midnight mass in his own parish of Kirkwall.

His tenor voice was renowned in both Orkney and Shetland, where he had been adjudged best tenor in the island at the Singing Festival. He also had the Provincial's approval for singing in the chorus of the Orkney Operatic Society, of which he became secretary until his regretted departure. It is not everyone who, when officiating at a wedding, would move towards the accompanist, and delight the congregation with his 'Panis Angelicus' or sometimes 'Ave Maria'. Non-Catholic guests, of course, were particularly looking forward to this, and remembered it long afterwards.

The sad day came for his parishioners and for the whole of Orkney when, not long before the death of John XXIII, he was appointed first

Master of Novices for Scotland. At a moving little reception of the whole parish, about forty in all, in one room of the presbytery, after evening mass on Ascension Day in 1963 in the bright sunlight of early summer in the Northern Isles, he said very simply: 'I cannot tell you how sad I am to go.'

He was replaced as Orkney's Catholic priest, and as chairman of the Italian Chapel Preservation Committee, by Father Bamber. Many people in Orkney will still remember Father Bamber, who was the priest at Our Lady and St Joseph's Catholic church in Kirkwall for twenty years. He had several short stays in Orkney and Shetland to relieve either Father Cairns or Father Whitaker so that they could undertake other duties, as he explained himself:

I was appointed temporarily to Kirkwall on the day before Low Sunday 1963 by Fr Provincial. I left Beaumont the following Sunday, 28th April, and after a brief interval I arrived here by plane from Glasgow on Friday, 17th May. Fr Cairns had a farewell party after evening mass on the feast of the Ascension 23rd May, and left on Monday 27th by the *St Magnus*.

On 15th July I received a letter from the Provincial appointing me to parish staff at Bournemouth. On 18th July I took a trip to Ronaldsay, thinking that I might not have another opportunity. Next day, four days after the previous letter, I received word from the Provincial that the various transfer arrangement had broken down and that I was to stay in Kirkwall until 'after the winter' and let him know then if I felt that I needed a change.

Father Bamber used to say that he had been sent to Orkney for fourteen days and that it took twenty years to find a replacement! He travelled frequently throughout Orkney, including the islands as well as the mainland parishes and saw great changes during his time. While construction work was taking place on the oil terminal at Flotta he travelled there every Sunday on a fishing boat to say mass. Among the many regular services that he held, was a monthly mass during the summer in the Italian Chapel.

Much new ground, in the ecumenical way, was broken during Father Bamber's time in Orkney. On 16th June 1985, he celebrated the first Catholic mass in

By the time Chiocchetti returned in 1964 with his wife Maria (holding the flowers) Father Bamber was the Catholic priest in Orkney and chairman of the preservation committee. *Source: Orkney Library Archives. Photograph by James W. Sinclair.*

St Magnus Cathedral since the Reformation, by kind permission of the Kirk Session, and six years later he shared a service in the Cathedral with Rev Ronald Ferguson, on Unity Sunday, 11th August.

When on the eve of his departure from Orkney he was asked by some friends what he would like for a farewell present, he answered, 'A return journey to Orkney.' Upon the news of his death in 1992, the *Orcadian* wrote:

> One of the most widely-known and well-liked people in Orkney for more than twenty years died last week at Mount St Mary's College near Sheffield. Rev. H. O. Bamber SJ, priest of Our Lady and St Joseph's Catholic church in Kirkwall for twenty years. He was eighty.

The most recent Catholic priest in Orkney was Father Ronald Walls, who died on 2nd January 2010, at the age of eighty-nine. He lived in the same Kirkwall street that his grandfather was born in, although he only moved to Orkney himself in 2006. During his long life in the church, he had met both Father Cairns and Father Bamber. At a meeting in October 2009, he said:

I celebrate mass every day in Our Lady and St Joseph's Catholic church and between April and September I celebrate an additional mass on the first Sunday of each month at the Italian chapel. During the summer numbers are swelled by visitors. In October I celebrate mass at the Italian chapel on the Sunday nearest to the anniversary of the sinking of the *Royal Oak*. Each year, the chapel becomes more popular as a venue for weddings and during the recent summer it has been used for a baptism.

18
Restoration

Caring for the chapel is an on-going process and keeping out damp is one of the main challenges. Gary Gibson has been a member of the preservation committee and a key figure behind the restoration work since the early seventies.

Really, restoration to the chapel has been a fairly continuous task ever since Domenico Chiocchetti's visit in 1960. However, whenever we have had to carry out repairs we have tried our utmost to keep the original work intact and, where this is not possible, to ensure we match what is there as much as possible. The Nissen hut was not designed to last for as long as it has, nor was it meant to preserve such rather fragile materials as are found inside.

Over the years quite a bit of damage had been done by visitors tearing off small pieces of the wall's surface in order, I assume, to prove that it was plasterboard! Also, there were a few areas where the plasterboard had simply disintegrated. We kept maintaining it as best we could but the condition of the ceiling became so poor in some areas that parts of it were hanging down away from the framework. You have to remember that this was plasterboard as it was during the Second World War, which was not of the same quality as modern materials.

By the early nineties, water had seeped in at various points to such a degree that the chapel had to be closed for several months while fairly major repairs were carried out. The task became a huge jigsaw puzzle.

In the damaged areas, we carefully peeled away the paper surface which Chiocchetti and Pennisi had painted and stored this to one side. Then we cut out the plasterboard that had rotted away.

This gave us the opportunity to check the structure of the internal walls. From the areas we could see, it appeared that quite a bit of the corrugated iron sheeting had rusted but that the main ribs and struts between the inner and outer walls were in fairly good condition. This, at least, was reassuring. A local joiner put in additional supports so that we could fit new plasterboard. The tricky part was to stick the many pieces of original paper back in place and touch up the joins so that it didn't look as if the wall had been repaired!

The chancel, as mentioned, is lined with compressed cardboard, rather than plasterboard, and parts of this were also in a poor state. One of the areas that had been affected was Chiocchetti's white dove in the centre of the chancel. Directly above this is a thick bolt that is part of the structure of the Nissen hut. This had rusted so badly that the dove had developed a rather brown tummy.

We kept the restoration work to the absolute minimum but something had to be done or the situation would simply have continued to get worse. We therefore took a section of the ceiling away and were able to remove all the rust from the bolt and paint it so that this would not cause a problem in the future. When the section was replaced I only had to touch up a very small area so that it is still Chiocchetti's original painting.

Gary Gibson was helped in the repairs by local tradesmen. The preservation committee has always included an Orkney builder (currently Alfie Flett), who provides expert advice on structural matters. Over the years, the dormer windows have had to be replaced completely, which meant the loss of Domenico's painted glass. The paint on the glass of the two lancet windows, either side of the front door, has worn away and it was decided not to repaint them in order to let more light into the building and so that the barriers the POWs had worked on could be seen from inside the chapel.

Gary Gibson also explained:

Kirkwall artist Gary Gibson had to carry out major repairs to Chiocchetti's statue in the early 1970s following an act of vandalism.

The area around the front door was badly affected by damp and we had an interesting challenge trying to preserve and catalogue all the pieces of the plasterboard's surface that had come away so that we could later fix them to new plasterboard.

The sand and cement coating that had been applied to the roof by the Italians, shortly before they were moved from Lamb Holm, did not provide sufficient protection against the wet weather and, after the visit by Domenico in 1960, a layer of bitumen was added over the entire building, apart from the brickwork and façade. This has been redone when necessary. The façade and statue are cleaned regularly of dirt and lichen, which grows in the pure Orkney air and they are repainted every two years.

Only a couple of years ago, the surrounding land had become so saturated during a period of heavy rain that water was found to be rising up through the floor in the chapel, which led to additional drainage facilities being installed in the ground outside.

The bell tower has been significantly reinforced. Ringing the bell proved to be too much of a temptation for many visitors and so the rope was removed some time ago and the hole in the wall inside boarded over. The original iron cross had rusted too severely to save and this was replaced by a replica, made in bronze by a local blacksmith.

The lanterns in the chancel were made by Sergeant Primavera from used bully-beef tins. The chains holding the lanterns from the chancel ceiling were repaired by the technical department of the local grammar school several years ago, which added some of the stars that can be seen today. Apart from this, the lanterns are as they were created during the Second World War. Those in the nave are made from a heavier metal.

Although people often think there is no electricity supply to the building, observant folk will notice that a dehumidifier is in constant use in the nave. However, there is no heating or light in the building.

Gary Gibson adds:

For many years the chapel was never locked but there were a few instances of people sleeping in it overnight and the committee decided this posed too much of a threat, so now it is locked each evening and opened in the morning.

John Muir had already stated that he had been known, on occasions, to drive to the chapel from his nearby St Mary's home in his pyjamas and dressing gown to open up the chapel in the morning!

The Wayside Shrine that can be seen outside, to the left of the chapel, was a gift from the people of Moena. The figure of Christ was sent over from Italy

In 1961 there was a dedication for the Wayside Shrine. *Source: Orkney Library Archives. Photograph by Norman F. Sinclair.*

and the cross and canopy were made in Kirkwall from detailed instructions sent by Domenico. The figure was originally multi-coloured but this did not weather well. Even the wooden figure has been the target of vandalism over the years, and at one stage this necessitated Gary's father Edgar carving two new feet. Since the entire figure has been stained black it has survived both threats much more readily.

'People in Orkney love the Italian chapel and there is a great collective will to protect it,' said Gary Gibson. 'The remarkable thing is that it has survived so well for so long, when a great deal of the building is actually quite fragile.'

19
The Italians Return: 1992

In 1992, eight ex-POWs from Camp 60 and Camp 34 made an historic return journey to Orkney, fifty years after they had first arrived on the islands. None of the men had been back since they had left in 1944 and 1945 and they were treated as honoured guests, with Italian flags flying from many vantage points during their stay.

The service held in the chapel was conducted by Monsignor Rossi. As a young priest, who had been ordained for only a year, he had been interned on the Isle of Man along with so many other Italians following Mussolini's decision to take Italy into the war.

The ex-POW association, which organised the trip, was made up of fewer than thirty members even at its peak. The association faced the difficulty of tracking down men who had ended up around the world following their repatriation. Men wanted to get on with their lives again after so many years away from loved ones and friends. Domenico sent the following letter.

Dear Friends,
The dream of a visit to Orkney by many members of the Ex-Prisoners' Association has become a reality, thanks to the determination and initiative of our energetic secretary, Bruno Volpi.

You cannot imagine how much I wish I could be with you on this unique and long-awaited occasion, but, as you know, my health will not allow me to undertake

Eight ex-POWs returned to Orkney in 1992, fifty years after they had arrived on the islands. Standing, left to right, are: Vittorio Fabbi, Primiano Malvolti, Dino Catelani, Arduino De Benedetti, Bruno Volpi, Coriolano Caprara. Sitting are Ugo Barucci (left) and Bruno Fugazzola. *Photograph by Ken Amer, Orkney Photographic.*

the journey. You can be sure that I will be with you in thought and spirit, and I will share with you the memories and emotions that flood back.

Nevertheless, I can tell you that my family will be represented by my daughter Letizia and her husband, who have willingly given their help to ensure a successful outcome to the visit.

Allow me to share my thoughts on this event, which is as important to me as to you. Everyone who takes part in this visit will enjoy the same friendship and hospitality which I did in the past, and you will surely return this friendship with the spirit of peace and brotherhood between peoples, which the chapel symbolises.

I wish to remind you of the words I wrote in my letter on departure after the first restoration as long ago as 1960. 'Dear Orcadians, the chapel is yours, for you to take care of and to love.'

For all these years, the people of Orkney have shown that they love our chapel and can look after it well.

Amongst the eight was Primiano Malvolti, better known during his captivity in Orkney as 'Shipwreck'. He returned to Italy after the war, worked on the railways, married and had four children.

Another of the men who returned to Orkney in 1992 was Gino Caprara. He had been an office boy, learning to become a building surveyor, when he was called up at the age of nineteen. By the time he was repatriated he was twenty-seven years old and paid work was extremely scarce. Gino worked for a while as a lorry driver then a taxi driver before getting a job as a land agent for a large farm producing fruit. After marrying his sweetheart Amalia he found employment at a security agency and eventually had responsibility for the whole of the province of Latina.

The return journey was an emotional one and it would be impossible to imagine the feelings of those eight elderly gentlemen, standing in a chapel they had last seen almost fifty years ago. The visit was filmed throughout by Jam Jar Films for its documentary on the chapel. Bruno Volpi made the following comments, as he stood alone in the building.

The colours are still bright. I remember as if it was yesterday. This twisted piece of iron reminds me of Palumbi and his work. I am amazed to find out that it is still intact. Some super power must protect this work. This place sends shivers up and down my spine. I remember how we found all the materials . . . looking for things everywhere . . . risking to be put in jail because of this. We stole things, but we didn't think it was a sin. We knew that it had to be done as a symbol of good will. They couldn't take it away from us. Despite the gates that surrounded us. We were prisoners but our culture was free. And we wanted to express it.

Several men were eager to learn what had happened to local people who they had known during the war. At the time, one of the most moving stories was printed in *The Orkney View*, a magazine produced by Alastair and Anne Cormack, who have given permission for the following article to be reproduced.

The two Italians, Coriolano Caprara and Primiano Malvolti, who had been stationed at Camp 34, Warebanks on Burray during the war, had said to us earlier that they would like to spend their free time in Burray and if possible to meet again anyone who might remember them. A phone call or two soon had the helpful Burray grapevine coming to our assistance with suggestions and we drove the men first to meet the Parks at Summerston.

There Coriolano pulled from his pocket a photograph, which he had kept for nearly fifty years, of a Burray lady and showed it to Donald Park. Mr Park immediately said: 'That's my sister.' He himself then produced an album with photos of POWs and there, in a group photo, were Coriolano and Primiano, side by side.

Memories, particularly of concerts in which Caprara had starred, soon began to be exchanged between the two Italians and the Parks. However, time was all too short and soon we had to go. It was as we were leaving that Coriolano said this was the house he had often visited as a POW — changes to the building since the war plus a change of name from Mission House to Summerston had at first confused him.

We next knocked at Daisy Wylie's door in Burray village to be greeted by Meta Mathieson, Daisy's daughter. She, at once, recognised Caprara and we were all invited in to meet her husband Peter and her mother. This time it was Primiano who brought out a photograph he had cherished since the war, a photograph of folk who had treated him with great kindness — Mrs Wylie and her late husband, and the teenage Meta. Like Donald Park, Mrs Wylie too had kept a collection of photographs of the Italians and sure enough, on one of them, were both Coriolano and Primiano. Once again talk flowed of times past.

The door opened and more visitors arrived — Peter's brother Bill and his wife Lena. They said to us: 'Have you come about the box?' We looked bewildered, so Meta went off to fetch 'the box'. This had been left behind with Mr & Mrs Wylie by another POW, Giovanni Di Blasi, when he was transported out of Orkney in late 1944 or early 1945. It contained all the letters he had received as a POW, drawings, photographs, notebooks and a few books.

Some of the beautifully executed drawings were of decorations similar to those seen in the Italian chapel and one showed a chapel (not THE Italian Chapel) in a Nissen hut. The family had kept the box all these years in the hope that some time and somehow the contents could be returned to Giovanni Di Blasi. Unfortunately, neither Coriolano or Primiano knew what had happened to him after the war.

Since the vast majority of the letters (over a hundred) were postmarked Taormina, Sicily, and an official number accompanied Di Blasi's name, we decided the best plan was to write to the Italian Consul General in Edinburgh, who had himself spent 4th June in Orkney with the group, to see if he could help trace Di Blasi on the basis of the information we could give him. Within a very short time we had a letter from him which said that they had traced Di Blasi's widow who still lived in Taormina.

Having telephoned her he explained that her late husband had left various letters and papers with a family in Orkney and she seemed delighted and very touched by their willingness to return these items to her. The content of the box are now back in Sicily with Signora Di Blasi, as the Wylies and Mathiesons hoped that one day they would be.

The Orkney View, 1992.

20
Fiftieth Anniversary: 1995

The return trip in 1992 was so successful that three years later, seven ex-POWs from Orkney returned with their families to the islands to celebrate the fiftieth anniversary of the official opening of the Churchill Barriers. Domenico sent the following letter, which was read out during the visit.

My dear friends of Orkney,

I am sorry I cannot participate in the celebration of the 50th anniversary of the construction of the Churchill Barriers with you and my follow prisoners. I am eighty-five years old and my delicate health prevents me from doing it, but my spirit and my thoughts will be with you on such an extraordinary occasion, which was so extraordinary three years ago, when my fellows went back to Orkney for the first time after the end of the World War.

At that time during the Holy mass, which was celebrated by Monsignor Rossi in the little church of Lamb Holm, the priest wanted to remember the dead fellows and above all the message of hope, which the Italian prisoners were able to express during their imprisonment. Today, you all are united to remember the huge work which was done by the Italian prisoners for the realization of dykes and roads, which link up your isles.

These two anniversaries strengthen the friendship, the esteem and the respect of two peoples and through the spirit of hope and brotherliness of the little church of Lamb Holm, they are the witnesses of a unique anniversary of peace, apart from the cultural and religious differences. The years of my imprisonment are still clear in my mind. I think I helped in the good state of the camp, though I did not participate in the construction of the dykes.

I wish to remember with love the commander of Camp 60, Colonel Buckland, who was a friend for us. He did all he could for us in arranging a lot of facilities and permission for the realization of the works. I would like to remember also the superintendent of the works of the barriers, the Englishman Gordon Nicol (I painted a portrait of him too) who shared relaxation moments with us, giving a prize to the winners of the contests. I remember also many other people of Orkney, who showed us friendliness and affection.

I wish to thank everybody, those who have the little Italian church at heart, preserve it intact in its structure, in the memories and hearts of the young generations. I thank also those who remember me with love, though a lot of years have passed.

Thank you. I'm with all of you.

Domenico Chiocchetti, Moena, 26th April 1995.

The event was well attended and received a significant amount of media attention, demonstrating again the huge and ongoing interest in the chapel. During his speech to mark the fiftieth anniversary of their opening, Alistair Wivell, at the time managing director of Balfour Beatty Construction Ltd, said:

The project was officially classified top secret throughout the war and was code-named 'Rockworks', so the whole story of the construction could not be told until the war was over. However, I do have an extract of the text of the letter of commendation received by Balfour Beatty from the Chief Civil Engineer to the Admiralty just after completion. It reads as follows:

'Gentlemen, the First Lord of the Admiralty has asked that his congratulations be conveyed to all concerned in the completion of the causeways at the eastern entrance, which he considers has been a very fine undertaking.'

Looking back after fifty years, it strikes me that this must have been a bit of an understatement at the time!

Bruno Volpi, who was secretary of the ex-POW association for Camp 60 and Camp 34, made the following speech:

The story of Italian POWs connected with the barriers' construction began in Egypt at a POW concentration camp in June 1941. All POWs arriving in Orkney from the camp were selected for their own professional skills. More than 1,000 selected workers sailed from the Suez sea port on board a troop ship, crossing the Red Sea and afterwards the Indian Ocean to reach Durban (South Africa).

After a fourteen-day stop for supplies and provisions, we left Durban for Freetown (Sierra Leonne) finally arriving on 10th January 1942 at Liverpool and were immediately transferred, by train, to Edinburgh where we were accommodated in a deaf-mute school for medical checks.

On 23rd February, we were allocated to the Orkney Islands and sailed from Aberdeen to reach that destination. 500 POWs were assigned to Camp 60 on Lamb Holm, 553 to Camp 34 on Burray. Immediately after our arrival, the men were set to work on the causeways, the transport road construction, part of a project to link four small islands as a military defence of Scapa Flow against enemy submarine actions.

After a short transient period characterised by a few incomprehensions, a real cooperation among the British staff led by Colonel Buckland, the Balfour Beatty technical representatives, and Sergeant Major G. Fornasier and Sergeant Bertone (commandants of 60 and 34 camps, respectively) started and lasted for the remaining period of the POWs' time on the islands.

The POWs carried out their jobs seriously and productively, even if the job itself and living conditions were not so easy. Many fell ill with psychological problems, some due to homesickness and the difficulty of getting used to the different weather, some due to the hardness of the work, many due to both conditions. To make their recovery easier the other POWs became conscious of a deeper spiritual involvement for them, this is the true reason for the Italian chapel building standing on Lamb Holm.

When the POWs left in September 1944, the major part of the work was completed, only asphalting and guard-rails were missing on the constructed roads.

Today we celebrate the fiftieth anniversary of the causeway's opening. While we voice our happiness at participating in the ceremony, we wish to proclaim ourselves to be very proud of our contribution to the Orcadians' economy increasing.

Many years have passed since then. Political and social conditions have evolved in both our countries. We hope that the evidence of our cooperation carried on during those difficult years should become an example to be followed by future generations.

Bruno Volpi, Secretary, Associazione, Ex Prigionieri di Guerra

Long after the fiftieth anniversary, Gino Caprara said:

There is one more thing I would like to add. It is that in spite of a horrible war, which caused tears, destruction, loss of young lives and grief, a link of friendship was born between our two countries.

I have a lot of sincere friends in several parts of Great Britain with whom, after more than half a century, I am still in touch, especially members of the Italian Chapel Preservation Committee to whom I and my comrades of Camp 34 and Camp 60 are grateful for having saved and treasured the chapel and the monument to St George. The politicians and all those who decide our destiny ought to think it over.

The years have taken their toll on these old soldiers and the ex-POW association for Camp 60 and Camp 34 held its last meeting in 1997, most of those remaining reaching the stage where travel of any distance was no longer possible. For years, Lesley McLetchie had kept several of the members updated about events in Orkney and she was invited as an honoured guest to this last gathering.

During the summer of 2009, three large envelopes arrived in the post. Lesley passed on to the author's keeping all of the correspondence, archive material, newspaper cuttings etc. that she has gathered over many years. Another of Lesley's poems about the chapel is printed opposite.

Comrades

Young men from Italian sun-drenched
fields and farms, cities and schools.
Clean shaven, handsome men.
The years ahead stretched unending
before call to arms
to fight in desert heat and dust.
A twist of fate brought you
to cold and windy Orkney
constructing Churchill Causeways
to keep out the enemy.
Building for yourselves a Chapel.

Now old men, the few, your tears
fall fifty years on again
as in rain and wind salutes are given
to those no longer here.

Which is the greater
the Causeways or your Chapel?
Your Madonna of the Olives
will one day confirm the answer
you know in your hearts.

Lesley M. McLetchie

21
Other Italian Chapels

Many chapels were built in Italian POW camps around the world during the Second World War, but most were pulled down in the following years or left to fall into ruin. However, there are some notable exceptions and they all seem to have extremely moving stories attached to them. The author is grateful to the United Churches of Chambersburg, the Chapel Committee of Chambersburg, Pennsylvania, for permission to reproduce the following text, which is used in their official chapel leaflet.

One of the most heart-warming remembrances of the World War II years, and the years afterwards at Letterkenny Army Depot is its chapel. The human interest story behind its conception and the recounting of the religious charity of the men of the Italian Service Units who built it leave indelible impressions on all who hear of these events.

A letter from BG Ray M. Hare, US Army Retired, Commanding Officer of the Depot from April 1944 to May 1945, tells the story which initiated the construction of the chapel.

The little church was constructed by Italian prisoners of war at no expense to the government. Material was salvaged from abandoned farmhouses of the reservation. The project was undertaken under very unusual and nearly tragic circumstances.

The prisoner-of-war battalion worked efficiently and cheerfully in the General Supply and Transportation Divisions of the depot each day except Sunday. In the evenings, however, when the men were locked in their stockade with nothing to do, some became despondent. I made it a point to personally visit their compound every evening. It was on one of these inspection trips that I discovered one of the elderly prisoners attempting to kill himself.

Investigation disclosed that this man had just received word that his wife had died in Italy. He felt that he had nothing more to live for. The man was highly religious and had spent his younger days as a master stonemason, building churches and other memorials in his native country. It occurred to me we might help this man if we could get him interested in building something at Letterkenny.

I invited the man to come to my office the next morning. There I told him that the depot needed a post Chapel and asked him if he thought he could design one for us. I could see that he was very much interested. He said that he could not only design the building but could build it. I placed him in complete charge of the undertaking. He selected his own helpers who would work as volunteers after depot working hours. His enthusiasm was contagious. The project seemed to boost the morale of the entire prisoner-of-war battalion.

The tower was built first using native stone from the foundations of the old farmhouses. The rest of the building followed swiftly. The Catholic community of the city of Chambersburg became interested and arranged for the dedication of the little church by a bishop from Washington.

Like the Italians in Camp 60, the men at Letterkenny were given no funds other than what they generated themselves. They used scrap materials from the depot and raised money to purchase items such as light fixtures, new bricks, linoleum, paint . . . even cement, something their countrymen held in Orkney would surely have been happy to donate.

Stained-glass windows were purchased from a fund raised by some of the officers on the post. The belfry of the chapel is sixty-five feet high, about six feet square and built of stone blocks. There is a balcony to the rear but the most striking feature of the interior is a semi-domed chancel.

The chapel was closed shortly after the Second World War but reopened in 1963 following considerable refurbishment, and a series of army chaplains ensured constant and regular use. However, by the mid-nineties the Letterkenny Army Depot was being considered for downsizing. Following many years of discussion and evaluation, the deed to the chapel was transferred in 2003 for US$1 to the United Churches of the Chambersburg Area, thus saving the chapel for the future.

There are other chapels in America that were built by Italian POWs. In West Texas there is a beautiful chapel about five miles from the town of Hereford. Camp Hereford consisted of four compounds spread over an area of 165 acres and housed Italian POWs between 1943 and 1946. At its peak, it held more than 3,800 men.

During their captivity five Italians died and to honour their memory the men asked if they could build a chapel near to the graves of their comrades. Permission was given and the Italians built the ten-foot square chapel in a couple of weeks, paying for materials themselves. Several Hereford people still own paintings and mementos left to them by the Italians. A few remained behind after the war and married local women.

The memorial stone for the five Italians who died in Camp Hereford. *Photograph courtesy of the Hereford Brand newspaper.*

Often referred to as the 'Chapel in the Meadow', the tiny chapel in Atterbury, Indiana, was built by Italian POWs during 1943. After the war the building

The interior of the Italian chapel in Henllan. *Photograph by Molly Arbuthnott.*

fell into a very poor state of repair but, during the 1980s, the Italian Heritage Society, the Indiana National Guard and private individuals worked together to save the chapel and it was gradually restored inside and out.

The story behind the Church of the Sacred Heart in Henllan, West Wales, is equally moving. Around 1,000 Italian POWs arrived at Camp 70 in Henllan Bridge during July 1943, having been captured during the North African campaigns.

Although what money they had was taken off them upon their arrival (POWs were not allowed to hold real money) they did not encounter the harsh conditions and treatment that many of them had feared. Indeed, once they began to have contact with local people the POWs discovered a great deal in common with their Welsh neighbours, not least their love of family life, good conversation, music and singing.

The Italians wanted to build a chapel to fill a spiritual vacuum. There was no spare building, so they gave up one of their accommodation huts and men found space amongst their comrades. Their ingenuity knew no bounds. Tin cans were bent into scrolls or turned into intricate candlesticks and columns; side altars were made out of Red Cross packing cases. Flour and water were mixed to form a paste, which was used to glue the paper from cement sacks to cover parts of the ceiling and roof trusses.

The cement itself was obtained from a local contractor in return for craftwork, such as bracelets, cigarette lighters and picture frames. Timber and bricks were acquired from disused buildings nearby, while a bell was 'borrowed' from a nearby mansion, a POW carrying the item back to camp hidden under his sou'wester! In the chancel the men created an impressive dome out of bricks and cement.

Unlike the highly trained Domenico, the artist who painted the stunning fresco of the 'Last Supper' on the concave wall behind the altar was, at twenty-two, one of the youngest men in the camp and had only some basic training in art. However, he had great talent and with three brushes, a piece of string (for perspective) and 'paints' made from vegetables and berries, tea leaves and coffee grounds, plus tablets used to dye yarn from a local wool factory, Mario Eugenio Ferlito created his masterpiece working in the evenings by candlelight.

When the Italians were repatriated in July 1946, they were astonished to have the money that had been taken off them upon their arrival not only returned, but with interest, as this had been invested for them during their captivity! They were eventually reunited with their families in Italy, although some remained behind to work on local farms. Many later married Welsh girls, while some returned from Italy with their new brides to make a life in Wales.

In 1947, Camp 70 was used for a while as a resettlement camp for Germans and later as a secondary school, but it then lay empty and decaying until local engineer Bob Thomson acquired the land from the council. Amongst the brick and prefabricated concrete buildings, only one of the temporary huts erected for the POWs had survived intact.

In this hut Mr Thomson was amazed to discover rows of ceiling arches adorned with skilfully reproduced religious motifs, the walls lined with pillars, a dome-shaped chancel with a breathtaking fresco, and candlesticks standing on what appeared to be a marble altar.

His plan was to renovate and rent out the buildings to businesses. The chapel presented a dilemma. To save it from falling into ruin would cost a significant amount of money. However, to strip out what was there or knock it down . . . Like the demolition team on Lamb Holm, he left it alone.

'This little hut with the chapel just carried on,' said Mr Thomson years later. 'It stood up to all the storms and inclement weather and you got to the stage where you felt it was supposed to stay.'

His business prospered and he built a caravan site at one end of the land. Despite being built as a temporary structure — it consists of a timber frame lined with plasterboard, plus a corrugated asbestos roof — the chapel stubbornly refused to give in to weather or the passing of years.

During the 1970s, Jon Meirion Jones, the headmaster of Ferwig primary school near Cardigan, provided hands-on experience to his pupils on the meaning of an altar, which was an alien concept to many of the non-conformist Welsh children. He decided to take them to see altars in various local churches, including the ex-POW chapel. The children were enthralled and wanted to know more about the building's history.

By chance, Bob Thomson had recently discovered the address of Mario Ferlito from an Italian tourist who had been a POW in Henllan and had visited the area. The children wanted to write to the artist, but there were some misgivings about the reaction that might be received from someone who had been forced to spend the early years of his adulthood in captivity. Eventually, the letter was sent in May 1976. Mario Ferlito's response was warm and friendly. Thirty years after he had been released, he wrote:

I did not realise the mystery I had left behind and I could not believe that children of this modern, materialistic age would bother to study my work. In all those years it was the first direct contact I had received from Wales.

Jon Jones suggested that perhaps some of the ex-POWs could be invited back and the school parents took the idea to their hearts, many of them remembering fondly the young Italians who had worked on local farms. The result was that eight ex-POWs, along with their families, returned to Henllan in 1977 and strong bonds of friendship were formed between a small Welsh community and families from Italy.

Although the chapel is on private land and can be visited by appointment only, more than 3,000 people tour the building each year.

Mario Ferlito died in May 2009. At the time of his return visit he said on entering the church: 'Through the rainbow of my tears I could see the days of my youth unfolding before me like the pages of a book.'

Inside the tiny chapel in Kenya.
Photograph by Molly Arbuthnott.

There are other examples around the world. In Kenya, about thirty miles from Nairobi on the old road north-west of Limuru, sits a tiny chapel, which was built by the Italian POWs who were constructing the road. In Western Australia there is an Italian chapel in the Harvey district, about 90 miles south of Perth.

The chapel in Camp 34 on Burray. *Source: Orkney Library Archives. Photograph by James W. Sinclair.*

Of course, we should not forget the other Orkney chapel, in Camp 34. This chapel, also a converted Nissen hut, was completed long before the building in Camp 60, but was unfortunately knocked down with the other huts after the war.

22
Past, Present, Future

Domenico Chiocchetti died on 7th May 1999, only a week before his eighty-ninth birthday. Such was his standing at the time that several national UK newspapers carried his obituary. The following month a Memorial Requiem mass was held in the Lamb Holm chapel. It was conducted by The Right Reverend Mario Conti, Bishop of Aberdeen (now Archbishop of Glasgow), and amongst the congregation were Domenico's wife Maria and their three children, Fabio, Letizia and Angela. During mass the following letter from the family was read:

Dear Friends,

We are extremely glad to be here with you to remember our dear father, Domenico. He is here among us: he is as near as he was during his life and in particular the latest year. These years have been marked by the memory of your friendship, which was the best medicine for his unsteady health and an invaluable support for his spiritual well-being.

He had carefully prepared his departure from this world; his thoughts always went beyond the daily matters and, in leaving us, he said: 'Say goodbye to the friends from Orkney and to all those who loved me.' He also said to our mother; 'Pray to the Madonna of Peace. She protected me on many occasions,' and she was the recipient of his last prayer and thought.

We are now here together, sharing the same pain but comforted by the same feeling of friendship, confident that the message of the Italian Chapel is a message of peace and hope that everyone can share and relate to in our daily living.

We are deeply moved and extremely grateful for the affection you showed us in this painful moment as on many occasions in the past, and on our part we will endeavour to strengthen the friendship that links our two communities and will always love these places and your people as our father wished.

We embrace you all

The Chiocchetti Family

Maria Chiocchetti died in 2007 at the age of eighty-nine.

A few weeks after he left Lamb Holm, Major Buckland was promoted to Lt Colonel, but by the end of 1946 his services in the army were no longer required. He set up a small commercial stationery business, which he ran from his home in Shropshire where he continued to enjoy music, singing and practical jokes. Following the visit by Domenico in 1960, the two men kept in regular contact until the death of Thomas Buckland in 1969 at the age of eighty-two.

Sergeant Giovanni Pennisi set up a business as a decorator upon his return to Italy. He married and had a son. Giovanni Pennisi died in 1989.

Bruno Volpi died in 2008, leaving behind a son and daughter.

James Sinclair continued to take photographs until his late seventies and, when he died in 1984 at the age of eighty-three, he left a unique record of Orkney life that spanned some sixty years. His photographs of Domenico and Giuseppe, and the group shot of some of the craftsmen in front of the façade, are probably the two most famous images ever taken of the chapel.

Ernest Marwick became a well-known Orkney author and a writer for both the *Orcadian* and *Orkney Herald* newspapers. Following Domenico's visit in 1960 he remained in regular contact with the artist until his death in 1977.

Following the completion of the barriers Bill Johnstone was called up, joined the Royal Navy and sent to the naval dockyards in Freetown, Sierra Leone . . . where he was put in charge of a power station! He died in 1981, having run a successful concrete manufacturing business for many years after the war.

The small girl who was so delighted with the wooden toy made by Sergeant Major Fornasier moved, years later, to live in Orkney and Sheena Wenham is now an Orkney historian who helps to train tour guides on the islands. Her aunt Alison passed away on 30th November 2009, at the age of 102.

Tel. No. SLOane 3477 Ext. 582.

Any further communication on this
subject should be addressed to:-
The Under Secretary of State,
The War Office
(as opposite),
and the following number quoted.

THE WAR OFFICE,

52 Eaton Square,

London, S.W.1.

P/120265/1 (A.G.14.B./1)

Your reference ....

22 Nov. 46.

Confidential.

Sir,

I am directed to inform you that your further employment has recently been under consideration in the Department, and to regret that it has not been possible to find you further suitable employment.

I am, therefore, to say that since it has not been possible to find you further suitable employment there is no alternative but to relegate you to unemployment. Further instructions for your release will be issued by the War Office to the Command concerned.

I am, Sir,
Your obedient servant,

Director of Organisation.

Lt. Colonel T.P.Buckland,
Pioneer Corps,
c/o O.C. Pioneer Corps Depot,
Delamere Park Camp,
Cuddington,
Near Northwich,
Cheshire.

Copy to:- GOC in C., Western Command.

Major Buckland was promoted to Lt Colonel shortly after leaving Lamb Holm, but by the end of 1946 his services in the army were no longer required.

Shortly after Patrick Sutherland Graeme died in 1958, the Graemeshall home farm was sold to the Sinclair family, who had been tenant farmers on the land for many years. The sale included Lamb Holm. Today, the island is owned by Tom and Christine Sinclair. The quarry where so many of the Italian POWs worked was flooded years ago and is now used by a local shellfish merchant and also as a hatchery for lobsters, which are released back into the sea.

Many Orkney families treasure gifts given to their parents or grandparents by the Italians when they left the islands. The Mathieson family in Burray have the beautiful model of Milan cathedral, made out of matchsticks. Many other items can be seen in Orkney museums.

Today, the ties between Orkney and Moena are stronger than ever. The regular exchange trips of schoolchildren have often included one of Domenico and Maria Chiocchetti's four grandchildren, while representatives of the preservation committee have visited Moena on several occasions. Domenico's daughter Letizia has taken on the role of honorary president of the chapel preservation committee.

The Italians were correct in their initial assumption that what they were being asked to do was to build barriers, despite the quick reclassification by the authorities as 'causeways'. Essentially, the structures were designed and built as barriers then had a road stuck on top. The steep sides mean that there is no gentle slope to take the force out of the sea before it hits and 'over topping', where large waves break over the roadway, is a major problem during rough weather.

The situation has given Orkney Islands Council a fairly continuous headache for the last sixty-five years. To improve safety, the council fitted crash barriers during the 1980s along the outside edges of the road, but the sea has more than once ripped out sections.

Indeed, the force of the water can be sufficient at times to move the five-ton armour blocks, which can tumble down to the seabed. The casting of new concrete blocks is still carried out, although not with the moulds used during the Second World War. Each year, around 120 new five-ton concrete blocks are positioned carefully along the side of the causeway by a mobile crane, to replace those that have been displaced. The maintenance of the causeways costs around £35,000 annually.

It is only at barrier number four where nature itself has provided the solution. So much sand and silt have collected on the eastern side that new land has been created. The same thing appears to be happening at barrier number two, although at a slower rate.

A debate as to whether gates should be fitted so that the causeways can be closed off in rough weather continues to rumble on between locals and officials, with people generally not happy at being told they cannot travel if they want to. Judging the waves can be a dangerous activity and more than one car has been badly damaged when a driver has miscalculated.

So what is the future of the Italian chapel? A Nissen hut is designed to have an expected life span of around twenty years. One day perhaps, the entire building (which is listed Category B) may have to be enclosed to protect it from the Orkney winters. Everyone agrees that would be a great shame, when part of the appeal is to see this lonely little chapel on an island, defying all odds and elements to survive. Only time will tell.

And, as Alfie Flett pointed out:

Many of the preservation committee are beginning to be in need of a bit of preservation themselves! Some of us are talking to our own sons and daughters about taking on the mantle of responsibility for looking after the chapel.

Such a move would be in keeping with what the chapel stands for, connecting people of different generations and backgrounds, different beliefs and nationalities. John Muir said:

The Italian chapel is one of the most visited tourist attractions in Orkney and is admired by locals and visitors throughout the world. This is apparent from the many moving comments in the visitor book: 'Out of darkness come beauty', 'A tribute to man's creativity and goodness' and, from a child, simply 'Cool'. During 2009, there were fourteen weddings and couples have come from as far away as New Zealand to be married in the chapel.

It is loved, admired and held in the highest esteem by virtually everyone who crosses the threshold. The chapel represents an extraordinary, inspiring story and I think the preservation committee all feel honoured to play their part in keeping it safe for the future.

In Italy, Alberto Pizzi spent a considerable time tracing Domenico's family so that he could discuss and learn about the experiences of their respective fathers.

'The chapel is a moving, never-ending story,' said Alberto.

He is right. One feels that even if the chapel no longer existed, the message of peace and hope that it represents would go on. But while there is a chapel preservation committee of such dedicated Orkney folk, one cannot help but feel confident about the building's future. To borrow a line from *The Italian Chapel*:

The chapel remains, fragile and immortal, a symbol of peace and hope from people long gone for those yet to come.

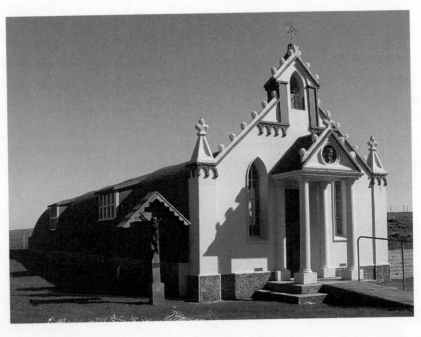

SOURCES

Aberdeen City Archives

Aberdeen Maritime Museum

Ken Amer, Orkney Photographic

John Andrew, Balfour Beatty Civil Engineering Ltd

Molly Arbuthnott

BBC

Balfour Beatty

Sam Moore Barlow, artist, blacksmith

Anne Baxter

British Museum

Camp Atterbury Veteran's Memorial Museum, Indiana

Coriolano 'Gino' Caprara, WW2 POW, Camp 34

Alastair and Anne Cormack, authors of *Bolsters Blocks Barriers* and *The Orkney View*

Daily Express

Daily Mirror

Guido DeBonis, WW2 POW, Camp 60

Margaret De Vitto, widow of Michele De Vitto, WW2 POW, Camp 60

Gina Ellis, daughter of Sergeant Major Fornasier, WW2 POW, Camp 60

Eddie Farrell, *The Hereford Brand*, West Texas

Alfie Flett, Chapel Preservation Committee

Letizia Fonti, daughter of Domenico Chiocchetti, WW2 POW, Camp 60

Gary Gibson, Chapel Preservation Committee

David Goodman, Letterkenny, USA

Robert Hall, Orcadian, son of Stanley Hall

Margaret Hogarth, daughter of Orcadian Thomas A. Thomson

Fran Flett Hollinrake, Orkney tour guide

Alf Hutcheon, Orcadian, ex-Balfour Beatty employee

Italian Chapel Preservation Committee

Jesuit Archives, British Province

Rosemay Johnstone, Orcadian, daughter of Bill Johnstone

Jon Meirion Jones, author of *Y Llinyn Arian*

Kirkwall Museum

Lesley McLetchie, Orcadian

Willie Mowatt, MBE, Orkney blacksmith

John Muir, Chapel Preservation Committee

Tom Muir, Orkney Museum

National Archives

National Maritime Museum

Tom O'Brien, Vision Orkney Photographers

Orkney Islands Council

Orkney Library Archives

Giuseppe 'Pino' Palumbi, grandson of Giuseppe Palumbi, WW2 POW,
   Camp 60

Renato Palumbi, son of Giuseppe Palumbi, WW2 POW, Camp 60

Roberto Pendini, WW2 POW, Camp 60

Alberto Pizzi, son of Ugo Pizzi, WW2 POW, Camp 60

Dr Francis Roberts, Orkney tour guide

Harry Russell, Orcadian

Norman F. Sinclair, son of Orkney photographer James W. Sinclair

Tom Sinclair, owner of Lamb Holm

Alison Sutherland Graeme, daughter of Patrick Sutherland Graeme

James Thomson, son of Bob Thomson, Henllan, West Wales

United Churches of Chambersburg, Pennsylvania

Father Ronald Walls, Catholic priest, Orkney, 2006 - 2010

Sheena Wenham, Orkney historian and granddaughter of Patrick Sutherland
   Graeme

Aidan Weston-Lewis, National Gallery for Scotland

J. Wippell & Company Ltd

Alistair Wivell, ex-managing director of Balfour Beatty Construction Ltd

Fiona Zeyfert, granddaughter of Lt. Colonel Buckland, commander, Camp 60

REFERENCES

Association of ex-POWs for Camp 60 and Camp 34, correspondence and
  minutes.
Boardman, Stanley: article in *Yorkshire Life*, 1959
Bolsters Blocks Barriers, Alastair and Anne Cormack (The Orkney View,
  Orkney 1992)
Buckland, Thomas Pyres: army service records
Buckland, Thomas Pyres: letter to Ernest Marwick, 1959
Chiocchetti, Domenico: letters to chapel preservation committee and BBC
Chiocchetti, Domenico: article in the *Orkney Herald*, 1959
Churchill's Prisoners – The Italians in Orkney 1942 - 1944, James MacDonald
  (Orkney Wireless Museum, Orkney 1987)
Giacobazzi, Padre Giacomo: article in *Il Corriere Del Sabato*, 1944
Giacobazzi, Padre Giacomo: article in the *Orkney Herald*, 1959
Last Dawn, David Turner (Argyll Publishing, Argyll 2008)
Lynch, Colonel: Report on Camp 60 by POW Inspector of Camps, 1942
Nicol, Gordon: letter to Major Buckland, 1944
Nightmare at Scapa Flow, H. J. Weaver (Birlinn, Edinburgh 2008)
Orcadian
Orkney Herald
Orkney's Italian Chapel, Chapel Booklet
Padre Giacomo Giacobazzi, biography, Father Berardo Rossi (Edizioni Radio
  Tau, Bologna 1997)
Roberts, Ruth Winne: article 'Church of the Sacred Heart'
Santini, Celso: letter to Domenico Chiocchetti, 1960
Scapa, James Miller (Birlinn, Edinburgh 2000)

Scapa Flow in War and Peace, W. S. Hewison (Bellavista Publications, Orkney 1995)

Scotland's War, Seona Robertson and Leslie Wilson (Mainstream Publishing, Edinburgh 1995)

The British Empire and its Italian Prisoners of War, Bob Moore and Kent Fedorowich (Palgrave Macmillan, Basingstoke 2002)

The Great Harbour Scapa Flow, W. S. Hewison (Birlinn, Edinburgh 2005)

The Italian Chapel – A Twentieth Century Renaissance – thesis by Rachel Stuart

The Miracle of Camp 60, documentary by Jam Jar Films

The Navel Wrecks of Scapa Flow, Peter L. Smith (The Orkney Press, Orkney 1989)

The Orcadian Book of the 20th Century, Howard Hazell (The Orcadian, Orkney 2000)

The Orkney View, Alastair and Anne Cormack (The Orkney View, Orkney 1992)

The Royal Oak Disaster, Gerald S. Snyder (Presidio Press, California 1976)

The Second World War, Winston Churchill (Pimlico, London 2002)

The Wrecks of Scapa Flow, David M. Ferguson (The Orkney Press, Orkney 1985)

INDEX